ASK ME ANYTHING!

Strange but true answers to 99 wacky questions

ASK ME ANYTHING!

Strange but true answers to 99 wacky questions

Marg Meikle

Illustrated by
Tina Holdcroft

Scholastic Canada Ltd.
Toronto New York London Auckland Sydney
Mexico City New Delhi Hong Kong Buenos Aires

Scholastic Canada Ltd.
175 Hillmount Road, Markham, Ontario L6C 1Z7, Canada

Scholastic Inc.
555 Broadway, New York, NY 10012, USA

Scholastic Australia Pty Limited
PO Box 579, Gosford, NSW 2250, Australia

Scholastic New Zealand Limited
Private Bag 94407, Greenmount, Auckland, New Zealand

Scholastic Ltd.
Villiers House, Clarendon Avenue, Leamington Spa, Warwickshire CV32 5PR, UK

Design by Andrea Casault

National Library of Canada Cataloguing in Publication
Meikle, Margaret
Ask me anything! / Marg Meikle ; illustrated by Tina Holdcroft.

ISBN 0-439-98909-4

1. Questions and answers—Juvenile literature. I. Holdcroft, Tina
II. Title.

AG195.M449 2004   j031.02   C2003-905219-2

6 5 4 3 2   Printed in Canada   05 06 07 08

To Tim Berners-Lee.
Thanks for inventing the World Wide Web. *
It has made this writer's life
far more interesting.

Acknowledgments:

Thanks firstly to my good friend Margy Gilmour, who helped with the research, as did Dominic Ali and Tess Grainger. To librarians everywhere for being so accommodating. To experts Sylvia Branzei; Ewen Cameron at Massey University; Dr. Susan Crawford; Patrick Kennedy; Dr. Colleen Kirkham; Dr. Elizabeth Johnston, UBC Museum of Anthropolgy; Dr. Heather Meikle; Kirsten Parker at The Pacific Museum of the Earth; and Dr. Ulrike Radermacher.

Thanks to the patient folks at Scholastic Canada, in particular editor Sandy Bogart Johnston and publisher Diane Kerner. Thanks to Pat Hancock, the fact checker, and Dr. Eric Mercer.

Thanks to Noel and Mac for putting up with my home office mayhem and to children for asking great questions.

* See question #69

Contents

Are bats really blind?

And Other Astounding Answers About ANIMALS

Are bats really blind, and can they fly in the rain?

Garrett and Eli C., Augusta, Georgia

Bats are not blind — their sight is just dandy. The reason we erroneously think they might be blind is that bats use a unique system called echolocation to manoeuvre in the dark. It is like a sonar system — bats send out short high-frequency sounds, many of which we can barely pick up. The sound waves bounce and echo off objects and reflect back to the bat. The reflected frequencies are slightly different and the bats can determine from this change in frequency where to locate the objects. But this system only works for up to 40 metres, so bats rely on their sight too.

Bats have been given a bad rap — just think of rabies fears, even of Dracula! They are sometimes called flying mice, but the truth is that they are closer to primates or humans than to mice. Check out their arms and fingers! Because bats seem like flying rodents, they tend to creep people out, but many of them are really important in keeping the night-flying insect population down.

There are around 1000 species of bats, which make up a quarter of the mammal population on Earth. We still have to work hard to preserve bats, though, because they are so important in the food chain, and because they reproduce more slowly than any mammals their size on Earth — most have only one young a year!

To answer your second question, bats are the only mammals that fly, and, according to Bat Conservation International, bats *will* fly in the rain. However, the high humidity that comes with rain can affect the movement of sounds through air, so bats might have more of a problem flying then.

The wildlife department of the Toronto Humane Society sometimes houses bats in the refrigerator to keep them in hibernation until they can be safely released back outdoors.

2. How much water can a camel hold in its back?

Alex C., Ajax, Ontario

The idea that a camel might be able to hold *any* water in its back is pretty amazing. Amazing, but not true.

The hump is a very good example of adaptation. Camels need some way to survive the desert's extreme climate, since camels are huge, and the desert is hot and dry, with little food to be found. Camels get water from food and from whatever actual water they can find. But the amazing thing is that the camel can go a long time without a drink of water — a week in really hot weather and up to a couple of months when it is cool. If we humans lose more than 12% of our weight in fluids, we die, but camels can hold on even if they lose 40%.

This is partly because they have some built-in water conservation systems — what water they take in they use very carefully. Camels don't sweat much, and if they do their fur holds onto the sweat and uses it to help cool them down. Their very stinky urine is hugely concentrated, which means that they don't pass much water through that way either. And they have particularly small and clever blood cells, which continue to work and circulate even when dehydration causes a camel's blood to get really thick.

So is the camel's hump the key? Not for water storage — that is a myth. The truth is that the hairy, floppy "canteen" on the back of the camel holds fat, not water — up to 45.5 kilograms. It's there to live off when there is no food around. When it is really difficult to find a meal, the humps shrink, get flabbier and flop over to the side. That would take about two weeks. Amazingly, camels can regain their weight in mere minutes by drinking a huge amount (up to 100 litres) of water.

Camel Facts

■ Think goat: a camel will also eat almost anything.

■ Can you close your nostrils? Camels can. They need this trick to keep sand from blowing up their noses.

■ A racing camel has to be able to maintain a speed of 35–40 kph for 10 kilometres.

3.

Do fish ever sleep?

Karen F., by e-mail

For sure fish don't yawn, because you would need lungs and a diaphragm to do that. But sleep? That depends. If you believe that sleep means you have to have your eyes closed, then fish don't sleep, because they have no eyelids. But they can restore energy and save energy by resting. Scientists measure sleep by looking at brain waves. They know fish sleep because they can see the fishes' brain waves getting slower, and the frequencies getting lower, as they fall asleep.

Some fish hang around logs or on rocks so they even look like they are sleeping. Some sharks have to keep moving even when they're resting, because their method of breathing requires them to push water through their gills. From a human's point of view, none of these options sounds terribly restful.

- A dolphin — which of course is a mammal and not a fish — can turn off half its brain and rest it, but keep the other half agile enough to watch out for predators. There is even a word for this kind of resting — unihemispheric deep sleep. It isn't deep by our standards, though some species of dolphin manage to cobble together 7 hours of sleep a day, with the longest "nap" with half a brain taking all of 60 seconds!
- And dolphins don't just "wake" to watch out for predators. They have to stay alert enough to surface every once in a while to breathe — otherwise they would drown. Young dolphins have to surface every 2 minutes or so; mature dolphins can hold out for up to 10 minutes.

Why do dogs drink out of the toilet?

Noelle D., Edmonton, Alberta

Wouldn't you if you were a dog? Fresh, cold water right at your height — none of this bending over and lapping out of a bowl nonsense. In fact, if you were a dog, wouldn't you wonder why humans want you to bend over so much . . . and why they pee into such a great water bowl?

But your dog should not be drinking out of the toilet bowl. You know what goes in there, and you don't want your dog catching a salmonella bacterial infection, which spreads through human feces. If that thought isn't gross enough — one lick on your face from your precious pet after he's been toilet lapping and there's a good chance you'll get it too. Plus, the cleansers used to clean toilets could also make your dog really sick, or even kill him.

If all of this hasn't convinced you to keep the toilet lid down, here's one more reason. When your pet drinks from the toilet, it's impossible to keep track of how much water he's drinking. Why should you care about that? Because if your dog is sick, knowing if he's drinking too much or not enough water can help the veterinarian figure out what's wrong. So keep a bowl of fresh cold water around. (And if you are feeling generous, raise it up to toilet height. You can buy little tables with holes cut out to hold the bowls for just that purpose.)

Do birds have a sense of smell?

Marjorie H., Toronto, Ontario

They most certainly do, but unlike other animals, birds don't rely primarily on their sense of smell to find their mother or their dinner. Because of the superb qualities of the bird eye, birds use their eyes and their ears first, and then their noses. Birds' eyes are far larger in proportion to their heads than humans' eyes — up to fifteen times the proportional weight. They can have up to six to eight times better distance vision than we do. Birds' eyes are flatter, giving them a larger focus area, and they can have as many as five times the light receptors as we do. The result? They can see far better in a wider area and in much lower light than we can.

There is always an exception to the sight-over-scent rule, though, and it is the kiwi, the only bird with external nostrils way down at the end of its bill, so it can actually sniff around and find a meal. The kiwi can find worms by smell alone. That's a good thing — its eyesight is really poor. Other than the kiwi, most birds have a very small part of the brain devoted to smell perception. It's called the olfactory lobe.

Birds with really big beaks are often really great smellers. Some scientists with a sense of adventure tried pouring bacon fat on the ocean surface. It brought black-footed albatrosses (with really big super-charged seagull-type noses) from almost 29 kilometres away.

And what about the old idea that a mother bird will reject a nestling that has been handled by a human because of the human's scent? There is no hard scientific evidence to support it, and now you know why there could be some doubt: smell just isn't such a big deal for most birds.

6.

Where did the goatsucker bird get its name?

Sandy B., Toronto, Ontario

Put goatsucker right up at the top of your list of unfortunate names you have encountered. (If you don't have such a list, this would be a great place to start.) This is not the name of just one bird, but the name of a whole order, *Caprimulgiformes*, which is related to the Greek word for "goat milker." (An order consists of a group of similar birds.) These birds have drab-coloured plumage, are primarily night fliers, and range in size from raven to sparrow. Within this order are various species including the nightjar, the nighthawk and birds with another odd name: owlet frogmouth.

But why is it called a goatsucker? Because these birds (who have been known since ancient times) happen to eat insects that hang around goats at night. Perhaps because of their odd, overly large mouths, the goatsuckers were wrongly accused of actually milking the unsuspecting goats by drinking directly from their udders. The term goatsucker is slowly being replaced by a more accurate and apt name, nightjar. That's because the bird's strange, hollow, monotonous sound is jarring to hear at night.

7.

What is the longest recorded flight of a chicken?

Believe it or not, thousands of folks gather every year in Wayne, Nebraska, to attend the annual Chicken Flying Contest and to see how far chickens can fly when scooted out of a launch pad (a mailbox) with a toilet plunger. (The record is 13 seconds of air time.) But many other folks don't think this practice is particularly good for the chickens, so let's just look at the facts.

The chicken's ancestor, the wild red jungle fowl, could and would fly if it had to. Aerodynamically speaking though, there is a reason chickens today don't fly. All of the poultry family is designed for a life on the ground. The shape of their feet, and their small wings, don't lead to a life of flying about. Also, because of selective breeding, chickens have bigger pectoral muscles (or chicken breasts), which make flying more difficult. Some smaller and lighter breeds can fly enough to get them over a fence to raid a garden, but most just stay on the ground. If they need to, some farmers clip one of the chickens' wings to "ground" them.

NOW THAT'S A CHICKEN DANCE!
According to the Guinness World
Record folks, on September 1, 1996,
72 000 people at the Canfield Fair in
Ohio, USA, stopped whatever they
were doing and all did the Chicken
Dance, a favourite at weddings
everywhere.

~

What do you call a bunch of chickens
playing hide and seek?
Fowl play!

~

Why shouldn't you talk like a chicken?
Fowl language isn't polite!

8.

Can dogs watch television?

Nolan W., Whitesboro, New York

Dogs seem to be able to watch television. Or are they just listening? Observations from a student's science fair project showed that younger, smaller dogs respond more consistently to television than older, larger dogs.

Until they learn to talk, we'll never really know what dogs can actually see, but we're fairly certain it isn't as much as we can. Humans and dogs see things differently, and the television tube was developed for our eyes. Televisions are actually flickering (updating and lighting up the screen) many, many times in a second. This is fine for us because we can't detect the flicker, but dogs have a higher ability to detect flickering, so the screen must come across to them as annoying flashing images. Also, humans have eyes that face forward and decent binocular (two-eyed) vision and depth perception. Dogs have eyes facing the sides, and their depth perception is much lower.

We know for sure that dogs can hear the television — TV doorbells set off my border collie. If dogs' most acute sense — smell — could somehow get in on the act, they would be glued to the television day and night.

9.

Are there any other crossbred animals like the mule?

Raymond Y., Toronto, Ontario

There are lots of other *hybrid* offspring — that's where the two parents are genetically different. The best-known example is likely the mule, a cross between a male donkey (or jackass) and a female horse (or mare).

The mule was bred around 3000 years ago as an ideal pack animal. The horse contributes the size and strength, and the donkey kicks in the amazing sure-footedness and the really long lifespan. The resulting animal, the mule, has the additional attributes of putting up with heat better than a horse can, and needing less food and water. It's a win-win situation.

If you cross a female ass (jenny) and a male horse (stallion), you also get a mule, which is known as a hinny or hinney, an animal smaller than the donkey/mare cross. Like the mule, it cannot produce offspring.

This is because crossbreeding works best with animals from the same species, with each having the same number of chromosomes. A horse has 64 chromosomes and a jackass has 62, so they are able to produce a new animal, but one that can't reproduce.

The male parent of the crossbred animal goes first in the name. All zebra hybrids (which are also bred as pack animals) fall under the generic term "Zebroid," and are usually called Golden Zebras. Technically, they are actually Zorse (zebra stallion x horse mare), Ze-Donk, Zonkey or Zebrass (zebra x donkey), and Zony or Zeony (zebra x pony).

PLAYING THE NAME GAME
So what is a liger or a tigon?
Liger = lion male x tiger female
Tigon = tiger male x lion female

What is black and white, white and black, black and white?
A zebra caught in a revolving door!

Why is it called a funny bone?

And Other Bizarre Facts About BODIES

10.

Why is it called a funny bone?

Sarah C., Ohio and Tyler W.,
Whitesboro, New York

It's not even a teeny bit funny when you hit yourself hard on what people call the funny bone. And it's not a bone, either. It's called the ulnar nerve and it runs through a groove in your ulna, which is one of the two bones in your forearm. The place of extreme pain is in your elbow, where the nerve and the bones are really close to the surface. Since they stick out extra far, it is even easier to whack yourself on the funny bone. Believe it, whacking a nerve is far worse than whacking a bone. It's like a gigantic crazy session of pins and needles and pain all jumbled up, so much so that you might cry and laugh at the same time. That's one of the theories of why it's called the funny bone. Some people think it's called the funny bone because the other bone that the ulnar nerve runs through is your humerus bone. Get it — humorous!

11.

Do Siamese twins have the same DNA?

Sarah A., Chesterland, Ohio

Understanding how twins are born should clear this up. Conjoined twins — the term Siamese twins isn't used now — are always identical and have the same DNA. Identical twins occur when one fertilized egg splits in two, so there was only one set of DNA for starters. The egg splits to make twin embryos and, voilà; two sets of DNA exactly the same. Identical twins share 100% of their DNA and are always the same sex. Now pay attention, because this may be about you. Fraternal twins (the kinds that don't look the same) happen when the mother releases two eggs which *both* become fertilized. They can be the same sex or different sexes, just like any other sibling.

With conjoined twins, the separation of the one egg into two embryos wasn't complete. This is probably because the separation started too late in their development. They are still physically joined at some part of their body, like the back of the head or the side of the trunk. Some share vital organs like the liver or heart. In some cases one twin doesn't develop fully and can seem like just a tumour on the healthier twin. One in 85 000 to 100 000 births results in conjoined twins — so it is a rare occurrence.

Conjoined twins were once called Siamese twins because of Chang and Eng Bunker, the most famous conjoined twins, who were born in Siam (now Thailand) on May 11, 1811. They travelled with circus sideshows until they settled in the United States and married two sisters. They lived to be sixty-three years old and had twenty-two children between them — Chang had twelve and Eng had ten. They were very good marksmen and keen runners — clearly they figured out how to work together.

In order for doctors to surgically separate conjoined twins, the twins have to have separate sets of organs. Only three-quarters of the 200 operations since 1950 have succeeded, with one or both of the twins surviving.

12.

If people are always shedding skin cells, why don't tattoos come off?

Diane K., Toronto, Ontario

Wait a minute; if tattoos could come off, wouldn't your freckles flake off too? Something isn't right here, so first we need to figure out how your skin works. It's a bit like an onion with layers. The top several layers of skin cells make up the epidermis. The dead skin you see is from cells constantly dividing from the base layers of the epidermis and moving up to the surface to flake off.

Right below the epidermis is the much thicker dermis. Tattoos are applied by sticking a needle a couple of millimetres into your skin, which gets the ink all the way into the dermis. So even after all the superficial epidermal cells have sloughed off, tattoo ink remains in the dermis, which stays put.

Tattooing goes on in most parts of the world and has been happening since the time of the ancient Egyptians. Lasers have come along in the past few decades to remove tattoos, but they are terribly expensive, don't always work and might cause scarring.

So that snake tattoo you thought you'd love forever? How about a nice temporary version? They are cheap and will wear off in a matter of days, but still pack enough of a punch to shock your mother.

How come your tongue heals faster than the rest of your body?

Eirian V., Vancouver, B.C.

Gash your lip or bite your tongue and you'll find that indeed mouth wounds heal faster than anywhere else on your body. Your *oral mucosa*, or the lining of your mouth, heals faster than other skin. But why? Because your mouth happens to have the right combination of factors to make it an ideal site for letting wounds heal and growing new tissue. It has an excellent blood supply, and that blood carries the oxygen, nutrients and proteins you need. There are also growth factors, clotting factors and antibodies in the mouth, which, combined with the warm temperature, make the mouth a perfect site for speedy healing.

OUCH!

Is our tongue the strongest muscle in our body?

Lavanya K., by e-mail

The strongest muscle in the body could be either the tongue, or the muscle that moves the jaw, or the heart, or the *gluteus maximus* (the butt muscles). Muscle physiologists, the scientists who study muscles, say that the strength and the endurance of the muscle is going to depend on your age, your sex, and how much you exercise the muscle (that goes for the *gluteus maximus* too). Babies need very strong tongue muscles to suck hard enough to get mother's milk to flow, but once past that stage, people don't need such a strong tongue.

Comparing muscles like this is a bit iffy, though. An athlete will likely have a stronger heart and butt muscles, and a trumpet player will have a stronger jaw and tongue — that's all there is to it!

Why do my fingers and toes get wrinkly in the bath (and why doesn't the rest of me)?

Christie, Ontario

We humans are pretty much covered with hair everywhere but the palms of our hands and the soles of our feet. In many places your hair is so fine you wouldn't dream of calling yourself hairy. (A magnifying glass will help to spot the hairs on "non-hairy" spots like noses or fingers.) We have glands at the base of each strand of hair that make something called sebum. It is an oily coating that keeps our skin from taking in too much water, sort of like a light wet suit over our body. Skin absorbs lots of water when you sit in the bath, but here is a clue related to your question: the skin on the hands and feet has the thickest epidermis (the outer layer of skin) on the body, but neither the palms of the hands nor the soles of the feet have any sebum.

When the skin on our hands and feet takes in water (or, to use a technical term, when there is capillary action), the outer skin swells up but the inner skin layers don't. That means that there's an excess of the outer layer of the epidermis, called the *stratum corneum*, relative to the inner layers. The result — the "excess" outer skin wrinkles.

Something that results in a similar look happens in the dog world. Some dog breeds, like the Shar-pei, have a lot more skin on their face than other breeds with the same size head. To fit closely on the head and not droop like a curtain, the skin forms wrinkles. Imagine that wrinkly skin as the outer layer of skin on your finger, and the Shar-pei's skull as the inner layer of skin on your finger — the outer skin has "gathers" that the underlying skin doesn't.

Why don't the hands and feet produce any sebum? You wouldn't want to try grabbing things or walking with "greasy" hands and feet!

Want to try an experiment? Try coating one hand with oil soon after you get in the bath and see if the other gets more wrinkles.

What are you really doing when you crack your knuckles?

Laura N., Cambridge, Ontario

You are creeping people out, for starters. Very few things drive folks as crazy as hearing someone cracking their knuckles and popping their joints — except maybe running their fingernails down a blackboard. About one-quarter of the population has this extremely annoying habit.

What you are actually doing is pulling apart the two bones of your finger joint and letting a lubricating fluid, called synovial fluid, zip into the gap between them. Because you're increasing the space between your bones, the pressure on the fluid (which contains carbon dioxide) goes down, and little gas bubbles form. The pressure keeps dropping until the gas that was dissolved in the synovial fluid is able to escape as gas bubbles. It is the same principle as when you open a can of soda and the bubbles of carbon dioxide pop and crackle to the surface.

It takes 15 minutes for the fluid to build up enough pressure so you could crack your knuckles again. If you happen to be "a cracker," you will constantly be told that you will end up with arthritis. That's not true, but you are in fact pulling your joint beyond its regular range of motion, stressing out the ligaments and tendons in the process. Do it enough and it may not return to its normal function. You don't want to end up with a weaker grip . . . or lose friends and relatives by being so annoying, so stop cracking your knuckles!

What are goose bumps?

Thom L., Jeannette, Pennsylvania

Goose bumps are formed when the tiny muscles in your body's hair follicles contract when you are cold, making those hairs stand on end. This doesn't look like much on a blond child, but when our much furrier ancestors got cold, it would have been pretty impressive, because humans used to have denser, longer hair all over their bodies. The goose bumps fluffed up the hair, which trapped air and made an insulating coat around the body. With evolution we have lost this denser hair that we don't need any more, but we still have those "piloerector" muscles, which produce goose bumps.

As well as cold giving you goose bumps, there are a lot of emotional rushes that can trigger your autonomic nervous system's feedback process and give you goose bumps. Fear is the prime example, and this too goes back to our ancestors. A rush of adrenaline, the natural hormone surge we get when faced with stress, was useful for the "fight or flight" response. If someone were threatening to attack you, your "fight" response would be to fluff up your hair to look bigger and scarier. Think of lions or bears — or your cat! They still do the same thing. The expression "Don't get your hackles up" really means "Don't let your piloerector muscles give you goose bumps."

Some people find that when they get excited or sad or mad they trigger an emotion-linked autonomic reflex — goose bumps. Other such automatic responses to emotions are blushing, gagging and getting butterflies in your stomach.

What makes bruises and why do they hurt when you touch them?

Arielle G., Whitby, Ontario

Ecchymosis: that's the medical term for bruises. And if you have ever fallen off your skateboard or whacked your head on something, you know just how *ecchy* it feels. The purplish-brownish mess, which can also be raised and really yucky, is from where blood vessels have broken and blood has leaked into the bruise area.

To get even more graphic, a bruise is reddish or purplish-looking on the first day you acquire it — the true colour of blood inside your skin. Then over the next couple of days your body chemically breaks down the pooled blood cells and your bruise becomes more blue and purple. Around day six, things go green, and after that, yellowy-brown. For the most part, it takes about two or three weeks to get your skin back to normal.

You can speed healing along a bit by applying ice or, even better, frozen peas. Put the bag of peas in a towel and hold it on your injury to reduce the blood flow to the area and possibly reduce the size of the bruise.

 How come we have wrinkles?

Alex C., Ajax, Ontario

Wrinkles are part of the deal — if you are going to grow old you are going to get wrinkles. You could think of wrinkles as like rings on a tree trunk, sort of a badge of honour for the years you do service. You will earn your wrinkles. Some people inherit sensitivity to sunlight and therefore the tendency to wrinkle.

You can avoid having more than your fair share of wrinkles by drinking plenty of water, by staying out of direct sunlight and wearing sunscreen and a hat, and by not smoking. That's because smoking affects the blood supply to your skin's top layer, and it becomes damaged. Smoking can trigger the release of an enzyme which breaks down the elasticity in your skin. Losing weight or muscle tone also makes you wrinkle.

You can't avoid the major wrinkle factor: time. Gravity affects the skin over your muscles and it will eventually sag into little folds. Your skin cells start to replace themselves more slowly and the inner layer of your skin begins to thin. At the same time, the fat cells under that layer start getting smaller. And holding all of the fat and skin cells together is a network of collagen and elastin fibres, which begins to loosen and unravel. With all of this conspiring against you, you don't have a hope to avoid frown lines. So don't get stressed about wrinkles — laugh about them, and you'll get laugh lines, the most pleasant wrinkles of all.

How come when you put someone's hand in warm water when they're sleeping, they pee?

Been to summer camp lately? This is a classic practical joke. It works mostly because feeling or hearing any kind of water can make you think or dream about more water, and that tends to make you pee. It works in the same way as running water when you are *trying* to urinate — it often helps to get you going. Nurses in hospitals sometimes do this for patients recovering from surgeries where the lower regions have been traumatized.

Why does it work? No one knows for certain — this isn't the kind of topic that scientists have worked on much. But it seems to be a reflex. Warm water may trigger the parasympathetic part of your nervous system, which can relax your sphincter muscles. Ever put your hands in warm water to wash dishes, only to suddenly feel the urge to head for the bathroom?

The hand-in-the-bowl-of-water stunt doesn't always work, but if your victim is in the right frame of mind he or she will be changing the sheets.

Why do men have nipples?

Good question. Why women have nipples is obvious — to feed their young. We're mammals and — like other mammals, even rats and whales — we have nipples and we have hair. The nipples may be hard to find on some mammals, and the hair may be microscopic, but it is there. (The exception to this mammal rule is the platypus, which doesn't have nipples. The babies lick up the milk that oozes out of the mother's pores.) Platypus aside, why bother with the nipples on the guys?

It is because humans all start out the same at the embryo stage. If you get an X chromosome from each of your parents you will be a girl, and if you get an X from your mother and a Y from your father you will be a boy. Genitalia (ovaries or testicles) start to develop at five to ten weeks. But even before then, everyone gets what are called milk ridges, two lines of tissue running from your underarms to your groin area. Eventually these ridges mostly disappear, leaving just two nipples, although some people have three or more, all along where the ridge was. Nothing more happens with human breasts until puberty, when they become developed in females, but not in males. Nipples on men (and on every male mammal) are completely non-functional, just a reminder of how we are made.

Right after they are born, both boy and girl newborns can secrete a tiny bit of liquid from their nipples. It is sometimes referred to as witches' milk.

Why do you blush when you have a crush on someone, or when you get embarrassed?

Leona, Ontario and Tyler W., New York

Blushing is like holding a flag over your head that says, "Look at me, I am really uncomfortable here." Your nervous system reacts to stress in a number of ways, including blushing. Like goose bumps, blushing is an automatic and involuntary reaction to attention that you don't want. When you have an emotional power surge — when you get scared, nervous, embarrassed, shy, flirty (like when you have a crush on someone), or when you tell a lie, get angry or get upset — you can get stressed and become very hot. You're blushing! What is happening with your body is this: your blood vessels are widening slightly to allow more blood to get to your skin. Your face has the most blood vessels, so that's where the blushing is most obvious.

Four out of five people blush, and if you are a blusher, there's not much you can do about it — it is part of your wiring. It's also part of being human. One of the things that separates us from animals is the ability to blush. (Others are using our thumbs the way we do, and talking.)

Not everyone blushes. Women blush more than men; small children hardly blush. If your parents are blushers, you likely will be too. It's not much consolation, but know that studies have proven that if you blush when you are embarrassed, you seem more likeable.

For some blushers, sipping cold water when they know they are about to get into a dicey situation helps head off a red face by fooling the part of the brain that controls blushes into thinking "I'm a cool cat." If you are a blusher, what do you have to lose?

23.

Can you die from constipation?

Everyone is different, but if you go three or four days without bowel movements you are likely constipated. That's when it hurts to go, and when you produce hard and dry stools. This is a very common problem and you likely won't die from it, but you can get yourself into trouble if your bowels don't move regularly. Medical people used to advise eating your bran or cornflakes to stay regular. Now they are realizing that a simple leftover like cold potatoes helps keep you regular. So instead of carrying a doughnut to school for your lunch or snack, consider a spud.

You can get stopped up from sitting at a computer for too long or from generally being inactive. Also from not drinking enough fluids or not eating properly. As hard as it is to hear this, know that junk food and rich food are not your friends if you are constipated. Get your act together and your digestive system will thank you. Continue to have problems, and you could have them for the rest of your life. Have a glass of water, an apple or a couple of prunes! And relax; it will all come out nicely.

24.

Why do I get an ice cream headache when I eat ice cream too fast?

Haley F., Fort Worth, Texas
and Genevieve N., Richmond, B.C.

Some people call an ice cream headache a "brain freeze." Whatever you call it, about a third of the population gets this annoying blast of pain in the brain. It is what is called a referred pain, where you *feel* the pain somewhere apart from where you are *receiving* the pain. Why this happens isn't conclusive, but when affected people eat really cold food or drink extremely cold drinks, the nerves that travel to the brain seem to be stimulated by the cold touching the top of the mouth. Then the blood vessels in the front of your head do a quick expansion/contraction dance to give you a sharp headache. (It's not really your brain, but *brain freeze* sounds better.) The way it happens feels a bit like a migraine headache, but luckily an ice cream headache goes away just as fast as it comes on. And here is a fascinating tidbit: about 90% of people who get migraines also get ice cream headaches.

A brain freeze isn't anything to be concerned about, but is a weird feeling nonetheless. Don't like it? Slow down when you are eating or drinking anything really cold, or keep the food or drink far from the back of your palate, and you should avoid the whole phenomenon.

Why do ladies shave their legs?

And Other Cool Facts About CUSTOMS

Why do ladies and girls have to shave their legs and armpits?

Katie, Nunavut

No one *has* to shave. In many places in the world it's just fine to have hair on your legs or in your armpits. But in North America, those who want to get rid of it rip the stuff out with painful devices like wax, or submit to electrolysis (tiny needles zapping the hair follicles), or shave and shave and shave and pluck and pluck and pluck. Keeping gals smooth and hairless is a big business.

When we started to shave our legs isn't so hard to answer, but *why* is tricky. That's because there hasn't been much information about how women dealt with hygiene throughout history. In order to put together a picture of the history of body-hair elimination, you have to look at diaries, statues and paintings. Greek statues of women showed no body hair, and those women were considered full of beauty and grace. Their legs only showed if they were engaged in military or hunting activity. And you never see armpit or leg hair in old paintings — artists throughout history have ignored reality. Only in the past hundred years have nudes been painted that looked like real women.

Showing a real woman, hair and all, came along with the invention of the camera in the late nineteenth century. A 1913 movie likely started the armpit shaving business. *Mabel's New Hero* (also called *Fatty and the Bathing Beauties*) was filled with gals sporting the new sleeveless fashions . . . and clean armpits.

Razor ads began running in 1915 in *Harper's* magazine, shortly after an ad ran for one of the new sleeveless dresses, picturing a model with her arms over her head, showing off her hairless underarms.

The caption read, "Summer Dress and Modern Dancing combine to make necessary the removal of objectionable hair." Whether it was objectionable to some advertising folks, or whether women genuinely didn't like showing their hair — they certainly started buying razors.

Why do we shave our legs? Throughout history, women's legs had mostly been covered, so when women's legs began to show (as hemlines started going up in the 20th century), a movement began to get rid of leg hair too. By 1925 dress hems were at the knee, and bingo! — even though women wore stockings, they wanted to remove their leg hair because they didn't like the feeling or the look of it sticking out of nylon stockings.

26. What do you call it when you turn ten on the tenth?

Madeline M., Vancouver, B.C.

You could certainly call it special, but there are some names designated specifically for the day your age matches the day of your birth, like seven years old on the seventh or twenty-nine on the twenty-ninth. The most common term for it seems to be "golden birthday," but "champagne birthday" and even "royal birthday" are used too. Whatever you call it, it is only going to happen once in your lifetime, so take advantage of this unique situation to have a particularly great party.

What did the birthday balloon say to the pin?
"Hi, Buster."

27.

Why do grooms carry their brides over the threshold?

This is a weird one, as it falls into the category of a tradition, although it doesn't mean the same thing today as it did years ago. Way back when, grooms carried their brides over the threshold (through the doorway) to ward off bad luck, because new brides were considered to be powerful and doorways were thought to be full of power too. If the bride happened to step over the threshold starting with her left foot, or tripped going through the door, that would be very bad luck. But the taboo has no effect if she is *lifted* into the room — sort of like sneaking past the spirits that guard the place.

Admittedly, a custom like this is hard to swallow in the twenty-first century. So is the notion that brides were often captured, rather than being willing partners in a marriage. Carrying the bride over the threshold was sometimes the only way to get her through the door.

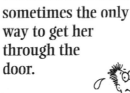

Who thought up "thumbs up"?

Eliza J., Kettleby, Ontario

Thumbs up is a gesture, and like head-shaking or rubbing one's tummy, hand gestures are a sort of sign language — a non-verbal cue. Some gestures can be taught to very, very young children (under one year). Some gestures are extremely handy when you travel, like sticking out your thumb to hitch a ride . . . unless you happen to do it in a country where it is considered a very *rude* symbol (sort of like telling someone to "stuff it"). This could get you into big trouble. However it came about, thumbs up is a hugely popular gesture.

Although it is grammatically incorrect (it ought to be "thumb up"), "thumbs up" has been generally accepted as a gesture of approval for at least four hundred years, and likely longer. It seems there isn't much more to it than the fact that "up" means good and "down" means not so great. And it might have had something to do with the phrase, "Here's my thumb on it," an old English saying that was used to finalize a contract or seal a deal. The two parties did a sort of "high five" with wetted thumbs.

The thumbs-up sign might even be connected to the ancient Romans' gladiator fight. The audience would *cover* their thumbs if they wanted to spare the life of a defeated gladiator who had fought bravely. That's what Desmond Morris, in his fascinating book called *Body Talk*, says. Through "mistranslation or ignorance," as he puts it, "this opposing pair of gestures eventually changed from 'thumb cover up' to 'thumb up.'"

Another hand signal that is used in the same way is what Morris and his colleagues, who wrote the entertaining book, *Gestures,* call "the ring." That's where you put your thumb and forefinger together to form an *O*, which is understood in many cultures as "okay."

While we're at it, here's another gesture that is oddly popular around the world. "Thumbing your nose" is when the tip of your thumb touches the tip of your nose and your fingers are spread out and pointing up (and sometimes waggling). Most school children will recognize this gesture as a tease, an insult, a way to mock someone or something. Sort of "Nyah, Nyah" with the hand. This one is often called "the five-finger salute."

29.

What's the story behind lighting the candles on the birthday cake?

Stuart M., Vancouver, B.C.

We have Artemis, the Greek goddess of the moon, to thank for the birthday cake. She got moon-shaped honey cakes to celebrate her birthday (Get it — moon goddess gets moon cake?) and the rest of us followed suit with round cakes to celebrate our birthdays. The idea of lighting one candle on your birthday cake for each year you have been around comes from the Greeks too. The superstition says that if you can blow out every candle with one breath after you make your wish, it will come true . . . as long as you tell no one what you wished.

There is also a belief that when you eat the words on a cake they will come true — so a bite of "Happy Birthday" will bring you happiness.

Another tradition says that the way your birthday goes will set the pattern for the coming year — so try not to cry on that day, or you will for the next 364 days too.

What did one candle say to the other?
Don't birthdays burn you up?

~

What did the Latin scholar say to the birthday kid?
"Carpe cakem" — Seize the cake!

"Doctor, I get heartburn every time
I eat birthday cake."
"Next time, take off the candles."

~

**Why do we put candles on top of a
birthday cake?**
*Because it's too hard to put them on
the bottom.*

30.

What is the origin of rolling out the red carpet?

Red is a powerful colour — the colour of blood
and danger and fire and roses. Red symbolizes life
but is also thought of as the colour of aggression,
vitality and strength. It is a colour steeped in
superstition and myth. But why?

Think: dye. Red textiles have always been
highly sought after, but before chemicals for dyeing
came about at the end of the nineteenth century, it
was incredibly difficult to get a great red colour
that was both light fast — didn't fade — and
washable. Three thousand years ago the
Phoenicians figured out how to extract dye from
molluscs (a snail called the *Murex trunculus*) to get
reds and the deep violet called Tyrian purple. The
catch was that you had to gather an enormous
number of molluscs, which made the resulting
colour so expensive that it was primarily reserved
for royalty. This is why the Roman Emperors wore a

toga with purple stripes to show their high rank.

Mexican cochineal beetles were crushed to get red dye, and Spanish explorers brought it back to Europe in the early 1500s. Red was the distinctive royal colour throughout the Middle Ages. It is still the royal colour of Great Britain, and the primary flag colour of the United States and Canada.

Red has come to be associated with royalty, pomp, circumstance and ceremony. When there is a ceremonial event there is usually a red carpet, although the expressions "roll out the red carpet" or "the red-carpet treatment" were first heard in 1934. As these things tend to go, the term has been adopted by the advertising industry, so stores looking for customers promise them "the red-carpet treatment." Good thing they don't have to go hunting for molluscs to do it.

Why are beans the musical fruit?

And Other Fun Facts About FOOD

Why are beans the musical fruit?

This phrase comes from a charming ditty:
Beans, beans, the musical fruit:
The more you eat, the more you toot! (or poot)
The more you toot, the better you feel,
So let's have beans for every meal!
I ate my beans and they were loaded,
Went to bed and they exploded!

This rhyme is said to have come from the time of the Depression, when there wasn't much money to spare, so beans, being cheap and a good source of protein, were a popular but often eventful meal. (As so often happens with oral history, this kind of rhyme rarely gets committed to paper when it first surfaces, so its origins are a little hazy.) But one thing is certain — eat too many beans, and you'll make music, hence the rhyme.

The following rhyme was collected in the 1960s in New York state:
Beans, beans, are good for your heart!
The more you eat, the more you fart!
The more you fart, the better you feel,
So let's have beans for every meal!

It may thrill you to know that the average grown-up passes gas around ten times a day. Eat beans and you've got a 500% better chance of getting gas. Mostly it's because of chemicals (non-absorbable carbohydrates called oligosaccharides) found in many legumes, that can't be broken down in the digestive system. The bacteria in the intestine try to break down these oligosaccharides, and in the process cause them to ferment, which can produce very smelly gases.

There are ways around the problem. Cool it on lima beans and navy beans, as they are the worst offenders. Try drinking more water. Before cooking, soaking beans for several hours in water that you change a number of times helps break down the chemicals. Or you could take Beano, a product with an enzyme that may help break down the chemical and prevent the stinky gas. But it doesn't work for everyone.

You will notice, however, that beans aren't the only musical food. Broccoli, cabbage and cauliflower all contain some amounts of oligosaccharides too. The catch is that all these foods are very good for you, so you don't want to avoid them. But you might have to get used to them, or at least work up to the amount you eat.

PASSING GAS, BY MANY OTHER NAMES:
air biscuit
anal announcement
body burp
cut the cheese
flatulence
fart
fluff
stink bomb
toot
trouser gas
trouser trumpet
wind

32.

Who invented chewing gum?

Hannah L., Banff, Alberta

Yum, yum, gum. We can all take credit for our ancestors inventing chewing gum.

Humans are built to chew, and archaeologists have dug up masticated wads — complete with teeth marks — of whatever was available for our ancient ancestors to chew on. Tree resin, gristle, pencil eraser — we love chewing. It relaxes us, helps us digest food, soothes our nerves and prevents seasickness.

Packaged chewing gum, however, first showed up in 1848. It was made of spruce resin, something Native Americans had chewed for centuries. John Curtis and his brother cooked it up, calling it State of Maine Pure Spruce Gum, and despite the bitter taste, the low price got things moving. Then Curtis got into flavoured paraffin wax gums.

Around that time an exiled Mexican general, Antonio Lopez de Santa Anna, brought a huge chunk of chicle with him when he settled on Staten Island, New York. (*Chicle* is the name of the gum made from the latex that's extracted from the tropical sapodilla tree, *Manilkara zapota*.) Santa Anna showed it to Thomas Adams, a former photographer and inventor, who imported more chicle to sell. A few years later, in 1871, Thomas Adams received the first patent to produce a gum-making machine. Chicle was better than wax . . . which was better than spruce gum . . . but none of them tasted great. Adding flavour helped. Adams's key ingredient was licorice flavouring — Black Jack, which you can still find today, was born.

A soap salesman called William Wrigley Jr. got into the act in the 1890s and his early inventions, Wrigley's Juicy Fruit and Spearmint, have been perpetual bestsellers ever since they hit the market in 1893.

Frank Fleer came up with bubblegum in 1906, although he and brother Henry's first attempts were disastrous. Even the name was a problem: Blibber-Blubber Bubble Gum. The gum was so wet you were blibbering and blubbering when you chewed it, and only turpentine and scrubbing would get the sticky mess off your skin. They never sold it. It took until 1928 for the company accountant, Walter Diemers, who was playing around with the recipe, to get it right.

And why is it always pink? Because that was the only colouring left when Mr. Diemers first made a successful batch of Dubble Bubble. Henry Fleer had an easier time. He put a hard candy coating around chicle to make the Chiclet.

It is hard to be discreet when you are smacking away at a juicy wad of gum. Of course the etiquette books of the day loved to hate gum-chewers. They called gum chewing vulgar and encouraged chewers to limit the gusto. Today Miss Manners calls gum chewing a pleasure that is never proper.

Tasty, though. Yum, yum, gum.

Baseball cards were packaged with tobacco until 1933, when the Goudy Gum Company got into the act and produced 239 cards to go with their "Big League Chewing Gum." If you had a complete set of those cards today they could be worth nearly $100,000.

33.

Who invented peanut butter?

Gabe L., Banff, Alberta

If you guessed that a child invented peanut butter, you are wrong. It wasn't even invented *for* children! Despite that, peanut butter has become the yummy brown glue that holds kids everywhere together.

Peanuts have been around since prehistoric times. They're not really nuts, but legumes that grow below ground. Ground-up peanuts have been used in cooking for centuries: we enjoy the delicious Indonesian satay sauce and African peanut stew. Peanuts came to the United States from South America in the 1700s and were used to feed chickens, the poor and the slaves. They were called goobers, from the Bantu word *nguha* (ground nut). In the 1880s circus showman P.T. Barnum came up with nickel-size bags of roasted peanuts to sell at the circus, and they were a huge hit.

In 1890 two physicians came to the same conclusion about peanut butter at the same time. An unknown St. Louis physician figured out that grinding peanuts in his kitchen grinder and spreading the mixture on bread made a great high-protein meat substitute for elderly patients with no teeth. At the same time another doctor, John Harvey Kellogg (of the cereal company family), was looking for vegetarian foods for patients at the sanatorium where he worked. Kellogg and his brother put 4.5 kilograms of roasted peanuts in a pillowcase and pounded them a bit to loosen the hulls, then fed them through grain rollers to make peanut butter. Kellogg was a fanatic about the stuff, and even published a book about it called *More Nuts — Less Meat*. This was the beginning of what has become a big sticky business.

The credit for peanut butter most often goes to George Washington Carver from Alabama — but that wasn't until 1896, six years after the other two men. Carver was researching the lowly peanut, and made peanut ice cream and peanut butter cookies and by-products like mayonnaise, cheese and soap — even paper made from the peanut skins.

Each year Canadians eat over 1.7 kilograms of peanuts per person. Americans, according to some sources, eat even more.

While it is too high in calories for most adults to indulge in much, peanut butter is an ideal food for children. It's relatively economical. About 45 mL of natural (unsalted and unsweetened) peanut butter contains 4.5 g of protein, all the essential amino acids your body needs, and small amounts of the elements iron and zinc. Peanut butter builds brains and tastes great.

34. What percentage of kids are allergic to peanut butter?

Peanut and other nut allergies affect about 1% of the population. Unfortunately, the peanut allergy is one of the most common food allergies. It can be very serious, but up to 25% of peanut allergy sufferers grow out of it as adults, so re-testing is recommended.

You may have heard at school about kids who are allergic to peanuts, so you don't take peanut butter sandwiches for lunch. It goes further than that — if someone is severely allergic, even a tiny trace (1/44,000 of a peanut) can give them hives or make it hard for them to breathe. It is really difficult but absolutely necessary for these people to avoid peanuts, so you are being socially responsible by not including PB and J in your lunch.

35.

How long ago were potato chips eaten?

Nicky W., Hamilton, Ontario

By me? Yesterday. But for everyone else — it all started not too long ago at all, just about 150 years. That may seem like a long time, but when you consider that folks have been growing potatoes for at least 4500 years, it took the world a while to figure out how to deep-fry them.

French fries came first. They had been popular in France since the 1700s, and came to America with Thomas Jefferson after his stint as an ambassador in France. But how do we get from there to potato chips?

The story goes that one night in 1853 at a fancy resort in Saratoga Springs, New York, a wealthy diner sent back his French fries, claiming they were too thick. The chef, a Native American named George Crum, tried to make a thinner fry, but the picky patron sent those back too.

So then Crum got really fed up and sliced a potato so finely you couldn't even pick slices up with a fork. Surprise — the guy liked them. So did everyone else, and they soon became known as Saratoga Chips.

Crum went on to open his own restaurant, but potato chips didn't become a widely available snack food until 1925, when a mechanical potato slicer was invented that could cut potatoes 1.5 mm thick. Waxed bags came along right about then too. So next time you get to the bottom of a delicious bag of chips and see Crum's crumbs, remember this story.

36.

How many potatoes does it take to end up with a kilo of potato chips?

The folks at Frito-Lay say it takes almost 4 kilos of potatoes to end up with 1 kilo of chips, since potatoes have so much moisture in them. Get rid of the moisture by cooking them, and you are left with the solid potato chips. Frito-Lay uses more than 2.25 billion kilos of potatoes a year.

Sniglets are made up of words that one day might make it into the dictionary. (Rich Hall has a great collection of them in *Sniglets: Any Word That Doesn't Appear in the Dictionary, But Should.*) Here are a few of Hall's potato chip Sniglets:

■ snackmosphere: (noun) the air that takes up 95% of the space inside bags of potato chips
■ charp: (noun) the green, mutant potato chip found in every bag
■ cheedle: (noun) the residue left on one's fingertips after consuming a bag of Cheetos

37.

Why is root beer called root beer?
Matthew L., Mississauga, Ontario

Because that's what it is, a beer made of roots — it has its *roots* in beer! But it isn't the kind of beer North Americans expect. Here, "beer" usually means the alcoholic drink, which is made with water, fermented grain and hops. (The hops are cultivated flowers responsible for the beer's bitter flavour, which counteracts the sweet malt.)

The word *beer* can also mean a non-alcoholic drink that is flavoured with the extract of a root. This is a very old-fashioned use of the word, but there are three of these beers available today: birch beer, ginger beer and root beer. Root beers have evolved over the years. The recipe has included up to twenty-five ingredients including allspice, birchbark, ginger, cherry bark, sarsaparilla, vanilla beans, molasses, licorice, wintergreen and sassafras root, plus carbonation. Unfortunately, a cancer-causing agent was found in sassafras so the makers had to replace it with an extract. Most of the root beer we drink today has either an artificial flavour or includes wintergreen and vanilla.

You can buy a root beer mix and combine it with water, yeast and sugar to make your own home brew. Given the chance, this mixture could ferment and produce alcohol, but it would likely be nowhere near as tasty as your root beer. Follow the recipe very carefully though, because getting the yeast to make carbon dioxide and give you the perfect amount of fizziness in your root beer is a precise science.

Why does chocolate give you zits? And what *are* zits, anyway?

Diane M., Toronto, Ontario

Eating chocolate does not give you zits — never has, and it likely never will. Zits are acne, which tends to come on with the power surge of teenage hormones, mixed with sebum (oil) and bacteria. So what does that mean?

Everyone has hormones called androgens. They stimulate the oil glands in our skin to get bigger and to make this yucky stuff called sebum. Sebum is the fatty gunk — dead skin cells mixed with skin oils — that your sebaceous glands produce. All of this is normal, but if you are prone to acne, your sebaceous glands overreact to your seemingly normal androgens, and produce too much sebum. Blackheads occur where a plug of sebum and bacteria clogs the hair follicles in your skin. And if that isn't gross enough, if the blackheads don't darken with oxidation, they'll stay white and become pustules, or open up and become lesions or inflamed acne cysts.

The good news is that there is decent medication, and usually acne clears itself up in a few years. Everybody's different, but one rule is universal — don't pick your acne. (Do wash your hands.) And don't worry about diet affecting acne, especially chocolate. There have been lots of studies, and it's just a myth that chocolate gives you acne. In studies where everyone ate chocolate, most people's acne stayed the same, some got better and some got worse. Being a teenager is tough enough without denying yourself something as delicious as chocolate. Enjoy.

39.

What's the difference between a yam and a sweet potato?

L. Berzen, Vancouver, B.C.

These two potato-ish foods are constantly confused. Sweet potatoes frequently tend to be called yams, but the two are very different from a botanical point of view. And neither belong to the potato family (Latin name: *Solanum tuberosum*) at all.

If you put them side by side, the "true" yam is usually dark orange, with a distinct starchy taste and rough scaly skin. It is actually a tropical herb native to Asia and West Africa, where it is a staple crop. It belongs to the Yam or *Dioscoreaceae* family. The true yam can grow up to almost 2 metres long!

The lighter "potato" is the sweet potato (*Ipomoea batatas*), part of the *Convolvulaceae* or Morning glory family, which comes originally from South America and is grown in the U.S. It is lighter-coloured than the yam. To confuse things further, there are two variations of sweet potato. The really pale kind with red or magenta skin and white flesh is generically called Boniato or "Cuban sweet potato." The darker variety (most common and most often mistakenly called a yam) has thicker, copper-coloured skin and deep-orange flesh. Two favoured darker varieties are called Beauregard and Jewel. Sweet potatoes are available year round and they are popular throughout the world.

In the United States a sweet potato tends to be called a yam. And canned "yams" are usually sweet potatoes. Why this mix-up? When the darker orange of the sweet potato varieties was introduced to North America, African slaves called them yams (from their word *nyami*) since that was what they were used to, and the name stuck.

While yams are more difficult to find in North America, they are worth the hunt, as they are an excellent source of potassium. The orange variety of sweet potatoes are also an excellent source of beta carotene.

Why are hamburgers called hamburgers if they aren't made of ham?

Eliza J., Kettleby, Ontario

Because they came from Hamburg, Germany. Sort of. Actually, the original hamburgers didn't look a lot like a Big Mac. They were more like a steak. It all started with a group of nomads called the Tatars or Tartars, who invaded eastern Europe and central Asia in the Middle Ages. They liked their beef raw, and even today some people enjoy a dish called "steak tartare" (essentially, ground or chopped raw meat) that was named after them. When the Tatars showed up in Germany, the locals decided they preferred their pulverized beef cooked with some spices. The Germans started to call the fried or broiled meat a Hamburg steak, and took along this taste treat when they emigrated to the United States. The sandwich was introduced at the 1904 World's Fair in St. Louis and was an instant hit with Americans. You can now get a hamburger almost anywhere in the world, and although folks think it is an American invention, you now know better. Adding the bun is American, but the Germans can claim the patty. Oh, and frankfurters came from Frankfurt, Germany. But that's another story.

Why does it burn if I eat a pepper that is too hot?

When you think hot peppers, remember the name Scoville, as in Scoville Units. The more of them you have, the hotter the pepper. How do you get something like this named after you? Come up with something that needs ranking, figure out a way to do it and see how it flies.

Wilbur Scoville did just that, and since it was 1912 there were no fancy computer programs to analyse things. He asked a small group of tasters to eat different peppers and tell him how hot they thought they were. Of course, nowadays food scientists use high performance liquid chromatography (a computerized process) to get their results, but they still call the units Scovilles.

Where do you get that heat? The burning feeling comes from capsaicin, a chemical unique to peppers. And capsaicin knows exactly how to get to you. It goes for the special sensor cells in your nose, mouth and throat, making them feel pain. Then your body shoots out endorphins to try to let you relax, but they haven't a hope. Eat a habañero pepper and your ears will feel like they are blowing off and you will break out in a cold sweat . . . And your tongue? It hurts to even think of it.

What's the point of eating these hot babies if they burn your mouth in such a memorable way? Some people believe that in hot countries people need to perspire to keep their body temperature regulated and stay cool. Eating hot peppers is also said to blow a cold or sinus problem out of your system. Others, though, think this is utter nonsense. They simply like the taste and love the feeling of relief after they have finished eating hot peppers.

There is no disputing the fact that peppers are

low in fat, packed with vitamins A and C, and include calcium, phosphorus, iron and potassium. The taste is worth it all and you get all those extra benefits: what a deal in a tiny package.

If you are going to try hot peppers, know this in advance: you can ease the burn with yogurt, milk or sour cream. Bread or rice help too.

Cool Facts About a Quick Burn:

These varieties of Chili Peppers are ranked according to their heat or "pungency" level:

SCOVILLE UNITS	PEPPER VARIETIES:
0 – 100	Bell and Sweet peppers
500 – 1000	New Mexican
1000 – 1500	Espanola
1000 – 2000	Ancho, Pasilla and Poblano
1000 – 2500	Cascabel and Cherry
2500 – 5000	Jalapeño and Mirasol
5000 – 15 000	Serrano
15 000 – 30 000	de Arbol
30 000 – 50 000	Cayenne and Tabasco
50 000 – 100 000	Chiltepin
100 000 – 577 000	Habañero*, Scotch Bonnet and Thai
16 000 000	pure capsaicin

* The range for this section is so large because some Habañeros are as low as 100 000 Scoville Units, but others max out at the high end of this range. The Red Savina Habañero, for example, is 350 000 – 577 000 Scoville Units.

42.

I like using baking soda and vinegar to make rockets. What's the difference between baking soda and baking powder?

Mac M., Vancouver, B.C.

Baking soda and baking powder both help make baked goods rise. Baking soda doesn't work unless it is added to a mixture containing acid, like sour milk, lemon juice, buttermilk or vinegar. The baking soda reacts chemically with the acid to produce carbon dioxide (CO_2), which is released as bubbles — that's what causes the cake or bread to rise.

If you look on the ingredients list for baking powder you'll see baking soda (its chemical name is sodium bicarbonate or bicarbonate of soda). There are other ingredients in baking powder to make food rise, like cream of tartar. When you add water to baking powder, carbon dioxide is released. When you mix it into dough you're creating gas pockets while you mix. By popping the batter into the oven or onto a griddle, the heat releases more carbon dioxide and expands the trapped CO_2, making more pressure and swelling the gas pockets, which expands the food being baked. You get the idea.

Really fresh baking powder is the key to better baking. You can try this freshness test at home: pour 250 mL (1/4 cup) of hot tap water over 2.5 mL (1/2 tsp.) of baking powder. If the mixture barely fizzes, it's time for some fresh baking powder.

To make your own baking powder: for 5 mL (1 tsp.) use 2.5 mL (1/2 tsp.) of cream of tartar, 1.25 mL (1/4 tsp.) baking soda and 1.25 mL (1/4 tsp.) of cornstarch. (You can leave out the cornstarch if you are going to use the baking powder right away.)

43.

What is the difference between a fruit and a vegetable?

Ethan M., Hawaii

You would think that there would be a simple answer to this question, like: fruit has seeds or pits and vegetables don't. But immediately your mind wanders toward exceptions to this fruit/vegetable seeds/no seeds idea. What about peppers or tomatoes? Are they fruit? Yes, they are, at least from the point of view of botanists, the scientists who study plants.

Botanists will tell you that a fruit is the fertilized seed of a plant, which develops after the flowers are finished. By this categorization, all of these are fruit (although we commonly refer to them as vegetables): beans, corn, cucumbers, eggplants, sweet peppers, peas, pumpkins, tomatoes and zucchinis.

So what determines that a plant is a vegetable? Botanists don't even use that category. What we lump together and call vegetables are actually many things. Here's how botanists divide what *we* consider to be the vegetable world:

tubers (potatoes)
flower buds (cauliflower and broccoli)
stems (celery)
roots (radishes and carrots)
leaves (lettuce)
fungus (mushrooms and truffles)

There is only one vegetable that we commonly call a fruit: rhubarb. It is actually a stem.

Cooks divide the world into vegetables, which we eat with the main course, and fruit, which we eat for dessert or as individual pieces.

44.

I heard a rumour that there was once cocaine in Coke. Is this true?

Matthew L., Mississauga, Ontario

It's not a rumour — it's a fact.

Coca-Cola is now the most recognized trademark in the world. The name came from two of the syrup ingredients: *coca* from coca leaves (the source for cocaine) and the *kola* nut (a source of caffeine). Back in 1886 when a pharmacist brewed the first syrup, he put it together as a "brain and nerve tonic" and sold it for a nickel a glass.

There was only the teensiest smidge of cocaine in Coca-Cola — perhaps 1 part in 50 million — but once cocaine began to be associated with crime after the turn of the twentieth century, it was wise to lose the association. People even wrote articles saying that there ought to be a law against drinking Coca-Cola. So the producers started to use only coca leaves that had already had the cocaine extracted. Then they dropped the notion of their drink being a cure for headaches, and instead marketed it as a drink that refreshes.

Coke (as we call it today) still packs a punch . . . but a weak one.

Beverage	Volume needed to get the same amount of caffeine
Coffee	1 glass
Tea	1 1/2 glasses
Coke	3 glasses

How fast does Santa
have to travel?

And Other Hilarious Answers About HOLIDAYS

45.

How fast does Santa have to travel? Like, what mach? How does he manage to get presents everywhere on time?

A scientist named Roger Highfield wrote a book called *The Physics of Christmas: From the Aerodynamics of Reindeer to the Thermodynamics of Turkey*, which is a very cool read. He has tackled this topic thoroughly and figured out the following:

There are over 2.1 billion children under age eighteen in the world, and for the sake of argument, Highfield assumed that Santa would give to *everyone*. He would have to make 842 million stops, (figuring on 2.5 children per household) on Christmas Eve, travelling 355 million kilometres in one night. The good news is that, working with the time zones and travelling against the earth's rotation, Santa actually has forty-eight hours to make his rounds — a little over 1/5000 of a second to reach each house and deliver the presents.

This means that from a standing start, he is going from 0 to 4116 kilometres per second in 1/5000 of a second, an acceleration of 20.5 million kilometres per second per second, or 20.5 billion metres per second per second.

According to Dr. Highfield, Santa achieves speeds of around 6395 times the speed of sound (which is 330 metres per second) or Mach 6395. But he is not breaking any cosmic speed limit because the speed of *light* is 300 million metres per second. In fact, Santa is poking along at 1/145 the speed of light. Even so, the speed at which Santa has to travel is why we never see him . . . and maybe why he is so appreciative of all those snacks.

What is Mrs. Claus' first name? What's her maiden name?

Bev S., Qualicum Beach, B.C.

That's a fine question, and brings up another: What's Santa Claus's full name? Actually, Santa is a title, not a name. It's a simple way of saying "Sinter Klaas."

Santa Claus is the descendent of impressive ancestors. One, Saint Nicholas, was a bishop in the fourth century. He is considered to be the patron saint of children, and is said to have had a generous nature. In the twelfth century he became connected with a Christmas tradition of giving gifts to children. In different countries, Christians had their own version of Saint Nicholas, like Holland's Sinter Klaas. The idea of Sinter Klaas followed the Dutch who started settling in America after 1609. Over the years the name evolved to Santa Claus.

But that wasn't what you asked.

Mrs. Claus has had numerous handles over the years, proving that there is more than one legend to her life. It looks like Mrs. Claus was first introduced as *Goody* in an 1899 book, *Goody Santa Claus on a Sleigh Ride.* (*Goody* is short for *Goodwife*, which is really a title, not a name.) That book was part of a set of thirty-two books written by Katharine Lee Bates, who composed the song "America the Beautiful." Other contenders for Mrs. Claus's first name are Jessica (from the movie *Santa Claus Is Coming to Town*), Anya, Martha, Betsy and Anwyn.

Since no one knows for sure, I suggest that Mrs. Claus be known as Mary Christmas from here on in.

Why isn't Canadian Thanksgiving on the same day as American Thanksgiving?

In the United States, having a feast to give thanks for the harvest has been happening each fall since the year after Pilgrim settlers arrived in Plymouth, New England. Local First Nations people had been celebrating harvest ceremonies there long before the arrival of white settlers. The idea of setting aside time to give thanks spread throughout the American Colonies, but there was no set "day" for the celebration — it just depended on the state of the crops and what suited the community. In 1789 U.S. President George Washington declared November 26 to be a day of national thanksgiving. At the same time the Episcopal Church was pushing for the celebration day to be the first Thursday in November. In 1863 President Abraham Lincoln proclaimed the last Thursday in November to be the ideal day. Then in 1939 President Theodore Roosevelt bumped Thanksgiving yet again, this time to the fourth Thursday in November. His plan was to help retail businesses by giving them a little longer window for Christmas shopping, since many Americans tend to have a shopping blitz between Thanksgiving and Christmas Day. In 1941 the U.S. Congress made Thanksgiving Day a federal holiday.

The first "Canadian" Thanksgiving — though Canada wasn't called Canada then — was in 1578 in the eastern Arctic, when explorer Martin Frobisher celebrated the safe journey from England to the New World. And Loyalists who moved north from the United States after the Revolutionary War brought the Thanksgiving custom to Nova Scotia in the mid-eighteenth century. The Canadian

Parliament adopted a national Thanksgiving holiday in 1879, and moved it around almost as much as the Americans had done: from the last Monday in October . . . to the third Monday in October . . . to the same week as Armistice Day (November 11) . . . to its final spot, the second Monday in October, where it has been celebrated since 1957. Canadian Thanksgiving also gives thanks for the harvest, but is celebrated closer to the actual harvesting time. Many Canadians who have cottages use this weekend to close up for the winter after their big meal. That's because one thing that hasn't changed much is the idea of a feast, and some of the favourite foods — turkey and pumpkin pie.

48.

Who invented April Fool's Day and when and why?

Evan D., Calgary, Alberta
and Bridget D., St-Sauveur, Quebec

April 1 is an annual excuse for practical jokers to try out their best tricks on potential April fools. This jesting goes on throughout North America, Great Britain, France and Germany. There is a similar tradition in India, where the last day of their March feast (Holi) is heralded with jokes and general mischief. In ancient Rome, March 25 was the festival *Hilaria*.

So what's so hilarious about this time of the year? No one is exactly sure, but it probably has something to do with the equinox and the coming of spring (March 21). Nature has a tendency to "fool" us with great weather and then retreat back into foul days. And it might have something to do with the cuckoo bird (the fool's symbol) arriving in April too.

In 1790 this poem was written about the confusion of the origin of April Fool's Day:

> *The first of April, some do say,*
> *Is set apart for All Fools' Day.*
> *But why the people call it so,*
> *Nor I, nor they themselves do know.*
> *But on this day are people sent*
> *On purpose for pure merriment.*
> — Poor Robin's Almanac (1790)

The other explanation commonly accepted involves the calendar we use today, which changed about 400 years ago (it is called a Gregorian calendar now). In the 1580s the King of France, Charles IX, decreed that New Year's Day must be celebrated on January 1. However, some people just didn't want to change from the long-established custom of celebrating the New Year between March 25 and April 1. Those who adapted to the change in France began taunting the "*poisson d'Avril*" (the April fish or April fools) who continued to celebrate on April 1. (Unfortunately, the fish/fool connection has been lost through the years.) These "April Fools" became the target for annual practical jokes, and over the years everybody got in on the All Fool's Day act.

Every year people are coming up with trickier April Fool's pranks. Be wary of what you read (a lot of newspapers run bogus stories), hear and watch. But the old standards still work too. If someone tells you to watch out for the elephant coming up behind you, you can be sure that you'll be called an "April Fool!" if you look.

In parts of Canada, the tradition is that all tricks must be finished by noon, but in Scotland the tricks can go on for 48 hours! So wherever you live, keep your sense of humour . . . and watch out for that elephant!

April Fool's Facts

■ "The first of April is the day we remember what we are the other 364 days of the year."
— *Mark Twain*

■ Napoleon married Marie-Louise of Austria on April 1, 1810, and earned himself the nickname: *Poisson d'Avril* or *April Fish!*

What's the connection between gingerbread and Christmas?

Ginger is pretty great stuff. It's almost up there with salt and sugar as valued commodities go. Ginger can flavour your food and preserve it too, and it can be used as medicine for stomach problems, flatulence and hangovers. The ancient Romans were keen on it, but after the fall of the Roman Empire it became expensive and rare. By the eleventh century it was more readily available throughout Europe, and fifteenth-century spice traders made ginger even easier to acquire. Nuremberg, Germany, became the heart of the medieval ginger business. The city was even home to a guild of *Lebkuchen* (gingerbread cakes and cookies) bakers.

The taste is great, but the fact that gingerbread can be cut into all kinds of shapes — like gingerbread houses and gingerbread people — combined with its preservative qualities, allows for Christmas decorations that can be used for a month or so, and then still be a yummy treat.

SPEAKING OF SPICES
Salt was once such a rare and precious commodity that it was traded for equal amounts of gold. The word *salary* comes from the Latin word *salarium*, which was a wage given to Roman soldiers to purchase salt.

What's up with kissing under mistletoe?

It's a strange custom, that's for sure. And stranger still when you learn that mistletoe is a parasite — it grows on other trees, most commonly the apple tree. The Druids, who were the learned class of ancient Celts, regarded mistletoe as extremely swell stuff. They thought it was magical, brought peace and cured all kinds of things (they actually called it "all-heal"). Like holly and ivy, mistletoe was also green at Christmastime, so it made a special decoration.

The kissing part likely had its origins around the fourteenth century in Britain. In churches where the custom was not discouraged — it had been forbidden from the fourth century right through the Middle Ages — mistletoe was used as greenery around a small display of Mary, Joseph and the baby Jesus that would be hung in a small hoop inside the doorway. Visitors were embraced and blessed as they crossed the threshold, by the priest or by family members.

After some years, the Church decided that they weren't keen on these models of the Holy Family, so the "people" were removed but the decorations were allowed to remain. By the sixteenth century kissing got added to the doorway ritual. For a while the rule was that for every kiss, one of the white mistletoe berries was removed. When they were all gone, no more kissing. That custom got lost somewhere along the way, and the hoops were lost too. What remains today is the custom of kissing under just a sprig of mistletoe.

Who invented the peace symbol?

And Other Intriguing Facts About INVENTIONS

Who invented the peace symbol?

Nick A., Seattle, Washington

The peace symbol, which looks like a crow's foot in a circle, or a Mercedes logo with an extra line, was invented in 1958. Back then there was a huge campaign for nuclear disarmament in Britain. Bertrand Russell, the famous pacifist, philosopher, mathematician and 1950 winner of the Nobel Prize for literature, was the head of the campaign. He figured that the movement needed a symbol or sign for its big Easter march to Canterbury Cathedral, where participants were going to protest the Atomic Weapons Research Station at Aldermaston. So the committee hired Gerald Holtom, a commercial artist, to create a symbol. He knocked around lots of ideas and came up with a crow's foot sign. But it has nothing to do with crows and everything to do with semaphore, the signaling system that most of us forget after our time in the scouting movement (if we ever knew it at all).

Take an *N* for "nuclear" and a *D* for "disarmament." The *N* is an upside-down *V* in semaphore, and *D* is straight up and down. Put them in a circle, and you get the peace sign. Upside down, it's like an ancient symbol for death and despair. It also looks like someone putting up their hands in defeat.

Since February of 1958, when Holtom finished his design, lots of people have suggested other origins and have reinterpreted the meaning: the circle means eternity, and so on and so on. The peace symbol became hugely popular with the peace movement of the hippie era, and now a whole new generation has incorporated the nuclear disarmament symbol on their fashions.

52.

Who created the Oscars? Was it someone named Oscar or something?

Carmela, Victoria, B.C.

The Academy Awards were started in Hollywood in 1927 as a way of honouring achievements of members of the Academy of Motion Picture Arts and Sciences. That's the professional association of folks who work in film. This gang needed some sort of trophy for their awards dinner, and that's where Oscar came in. A sculptor in Los Angeles came up with a knight. He's standing on a reel of film with a sword in his hand. At first he was solid bronze, and now he is made of an alloy, britannium, plated with gold. He is 34.3 cm tall and weighs 3.8 kilos.

Why Oscar? It's a little unclear. One story goes that the knight looked like the academy librarian's Uncle Oscar. She told the staff this story and they started calling the little guy Oscar. By the sixth year of presentations, a columnist referred to what's officially known as the Academy Award of Meritas, as Oscar. The academy officially adopted this nickname in 1939.

What started out as a little award dinner for 270 members has turned into an internationally broadcast tradition for the 6000 members of the Academy. Over 2000 Oscars have been given out, most looking exactly the same, but in 1938 Walt Disney got a regular Oscar and seven mini Oscars for *Snow White and the Seven Dwarves.*

TAKE A BOW!

When she was six years old, Shirley Temple won the first Academy Award ever presented to a child for her performance in *Bright Eyes*, the movie which introduced her signature song, "On the Good Ship Lollipop." The mini Oscar came with the message, "This award is bestowed because Shirley Temple brought more happiness to millions of children than any other child of her years in the history of the world." That's a hard act to follow!

53.

What year was the bikini invented?

Dustin

The bikini was invented after World War II, when the world was at peace. People still had war on their minds, though. Women had been wearing two-piece bathing suits (which looked more like shorts and a halter top) since 1935. In 1946 a Frenchman named Jacques Heim designed the "world's smallest bathing suit." It was a two-piecer which he called The Atome, referring to the atomic bomb which was being tested at that time.

Then Louis Reard, a Renault car company engineer from France, got into the act. He went further and came up with what he called "smaller than the world's smallest bathing suit." But he couldn't settle on a name. Then, four days before he was to show his suit, the U. S. military set off a nuclear explosion near Bikini Atoll in the Pacific, and the name came to Louis Reard.

The bikini was so skimpy Reard couldn't find a Paris model to wear it, so he found a showgirl to introduce his outrageous fashion on July 5, 1946. The gimmick was that it could only be a bikini if it was "small enough to pull through a wedding ring."

Bikini

Ring

Pull

This was hot stuff — too hot to handle for many years. Even freewheeling Hollywood mostly shied away for a long time.

In 1956 French actress Brigitte Bardot wore the skimpiest of bikinis in the film *And God Created Woman*. In 1960 the now-famous song came out: "Itsy Bitsy Teenie Weenie Yellow Polkadot Bikini." The bikini wasn't really accepted in North America for almost another decade — not until 1965, when *Beach Blanket Bingo*, starring Frankie Avalon and Annette Funicello, was released. Since then the skimpy suit has gone in and out of fashion, but in one form or another the bikini is here to stay.

54.

How was Velcro invented?

Once upon a time a long time ago (the late 1940s) a Swiss inventor named Georges de Mestral went for a walk. He came home and discovered cockleburs on his dog and on his pants. He was dismayed at these brown things gripping stubbornly to his trousers . . . and then, being the scientific type, he looked at them more closely under his microscope. Those darned burrs had hundreds of tiny hooks and — what do you know? — the fabric in his pants had hundreds of tiny loops. When those hooks and loops came together — bingo, you've got Velcro. Generically speaking, you have a hook-and-loop fastener, but de Maestral himself came up with the brand name, Velcro, from *velour*, the French word for velvet, and *crochet*, the French for hook. In 1978 the patent for Velcro expired, and there have been lots of competitors ever since.

Originally hook-and-loop fasteners were just used for clothes and domestic items. Now there are thousands of applications, using hundreds of different types of fasteners — everything from the regular nylon variety which holds your pockets closed, to an injection-molded nylon style with stiff arrowhead-shaped hooks used in the automotive industry to hold everything together (cushions, headliners and carpets). The fasteners are inexpensive, strong, resistant to vibration and can be heat-resistant and fireproof too.

Why do we say "break a leg"?

And Other STRANGE SUPERSTITIONS

Why do we say "break a leg" for good luck with a play?

Nikul P., Toronto, Ontario

We only say this under certain circumstances — otherwise it is just plain rude. "Break a leg" is part of an elaborate series of superstitions used since the early 1900s in the theatre. Actors are said to be the most superstitious people around (next come gamblers, then jockeys and sailors). It's not surprising — live theatre is a chancy business. Actors figure that maybe there is a reason beyond their control why they performed badly or didn't get a part. If they can't blame luck, they'd have to blame their own acting abilities, and who wants that!

"Break a leg" is a negative sentiment. The idea behind using it is a very old superstition never to outright tell someone to have good luck. If you sent best wishes or good luck to your friends, you would tempt the Fates or evil spirits to do the opposite and do them harm. Also, by wishing someone good luck, you would be parting with the luck yourself. So instead, actors think they are tricking the Fates by doing the opposite and saying "break a leg." The phrase itself seems to be a mild translation of what German actors say: *Hals-und bienbruch*, which means break a neck and a leg. This superstition might have started with World War I pilots, then spread to the German and finally to British and American theatres.

Some Chinese parents worry that if they tempt the Fates by "bragging" about a new baby's prettiness or intelligence, it might bring bad luck.

Why is it bad luck to pass someone on the stairs?

Likely this superstition comes from back when staircases were very steep and poorly lit (or not lit at all). The chances of meeting up with an enemy on the gloomy narrow stairs were very good. Wider staircases and electric lighting have rid us of the superstition, but even today some people cross their fingers if they have to pass someone on the stairs, to save themselves from bad luck.

If you trip on the way up the stairs you are said to be in luck, and might even be getting married soon. In addition to falling down the stairs — which is doubly unfortunate because you will likely hurt yourself — tripping on your way down is bad luck. And whatever you do, don't change your mind halfway up the staircase. Go all the way to the top and turn around, or sit down, whistle a bit and then head back down. That should keep your luck intact.

57.

Why do you stir the plum pudding for good luck before you bake it for Christmas? And why are little prizes like coins baked into it?

Sometimes cakes are filled with more than sweet delicious ingredients (and calories). Your family may not do this exact thing with your Christmas pudding, but many of the cakes we eat on special occasions involve other rituals.

The ritual of stirring the Christmas pudding is this — everyone who takes a turn stirring makes a wish. That gets everyone involved . . . and also helps ensure that there is no bad luck in the home where the Christmas pudding is being made — which, if you are superstitious, is always a good thing.

Hiding "charms" like toys or coins or a button in a dessert is an extremely old custom. The person who gets the charm will surely get good luck.

You probably know the rhyme:
Little Jack Horner
sat in a corner
eating a Christmas pie.
He stuck in his thumb
and pulled out a plum
And said, "What a good boy am I!"

Jack Horner got the charm — or in this case, the plum. In other words he got good luck from the cake.

Other charms which have been wrapped in paper and hidden in cakes over the years are coins (which means you will have wealth soon), rings (marriage is coming) or buttons (no marriage).

Cakes themselves have also been used as prizes, and that's where the expression "to take the cake" comes from.

Why do you say "God bless you" when someone sneezes?

Marnie S., Qualicum Beach, B.C.

Sneezing is something that everyone everywhere does. Over the ages, different beliefs have attached themselves to this rather bizarre act — it is like an explosion from within, a big-time nose relief. There were Native Americans who believed that sneezing clears the brain. Maoris of New Zealand thought their god of creation, Tiki, sneezed life into the first person. Others thought sneezing took the breath of life away.

Every culture also seems to have a need to say something after we sneeze — to somehow acknowledge the sneeze, which was considered to be dangerous. Whether it is the German "*Gesundheit*" ("Good health") or the Roman "Congratulations" (these cultures thought that sneezes ridded the body of the spirits from illnesses to come), few sneezes go unheralded. The Romans took this a step further. They believed that keeping in a sneeze would essentially kill you.

Christians and others believed that when you sneezed the soul left the body, so if you asked God's blessing, the sneezer might be saved from the evil spirits or from getting the plague. That idea came from Pope Gregory the Great (540–604 A.D.). It made perfect sense at the time, since there was a horrible plague in Italy, and one telling symptom was relentless sneezing and then swift death. So the Pope encouraged anyone who heard sneezing to say "God bless you" to attempt to keep the plague from killing the sneezer.

59.

What's the evil eye supposed to do to you, and how do you stop it?

You've likely heard the expression "giving someone the evil eye." This is one of the oldest and strongest superstitions around. Your eye was considered the window into your soul; people thought that by looking into someone's eyes they could tell what that person was all about.

It was also thought that if you gave someone the evil eye you could make them sick, give them lousy luck or even kill them. So it was in your best interest to stay away from those who had these powers. This might be anyone with blue or green eyes, or eyes that were strikingly different from the eye colour usually found in the region. It was definitely best to stay away from anyone with two different coloured eyes, and from folks with deep set, uneven, squinty or crossed eyes. People with cowlicks and left-handers were suspect too. And some animals were said to have the evil eye too — black cats, all black birds (like magpies and crows), black sheep and rams.

Belief in the evil eye was strongest at the height of the witch hunts in the seventeenth century. People even put glass "witch balls" into their windows in the hope that they would ward off spells, and keep out the bad sorts and bad luck. These were 15-centimetre blown-glass spheres, often with strands and swirls of colour inside, the hope being that this "web" might trap the spell.

If you happened to run into a person with the evil eye, it would be smart to have an amulet — an object worn as a charm again evil — on hand. The best amulets were shaped like the eye of a toad. Or necklaces of blue worry beads, a red ribbon, a piece of coral, horseshoes, or something with the fleurde-lis design could help. People whose aim was decent could spit in said person's eye or over their shoulder. Or they could put their middle two fingers down and using the pinky and pointer finger, show the other person the "devil's horn" or "fig sign." Then they would be okay.

Was the moon landing just a big hoax?

And Other Weird but USEFUL INFORMATION

Was the moon landing just a big hoax?

Betsy V., Toronto, Ontario

You also asked about another point: that the moon has no atmosphere, and therefore no wind, but in footage of the moon landing, the flag is able to flap. How could the flag fly without any wind?

There are many reasons to be skeptical about a lot of things in this world. It is always smart to examine the facts and make your own decision. Here are some of the facts about the Apollo 11 moon landing:

- The whole thing was seen worldwide on live television.
- The flag: On July 20, 1969, the first U.S. flag was planted on the moon by Neil Armstrong and Edwin "Buzz" Aldrin. It's still there. And it was no ordinary flag; it was a lunar flag. NASA says: "The design was based on a number of engineering constraints. For example, to compensate for the lack of an atmosphere on the lunar surface, the flag assembly included a horizontal crossbar to give the illusion of a flag flying in the breeze." The assembly was sophisticated, but the flag itself was a regular nylon 1x1.5-metre version from a government supply catalogue. It cost $5.50.

It turns out that Armstrong and Aldrin had a few difficulties getting the flag up. They couldn't get the horizontal crossbar rod to pull out all the way. NASA says "This gave the flag a bit of a ripple effect," and later crews intentionally left the rod partially retracted. The Apollo 11 astronauts also noted that they could drive the lower portion of the pole only about 15 to 23 cm into the lunar surface. It is uncertain if the flag remained standing or was blown over by the engine blast when the ascent module took off.

In conclusion: you were right to pose the question — you don't want to believe everything the media tells you, just on face value. But the flag flying *was* an illusion that NASA says they planned. We expect to see a flag flutter, so they made it happen.

Why isn't there a *Q* on the phone keypad?

There is no *Q* because when phone companies used words or letters for the beginning of phone numbers, they would be limited by the fact that *U* has to follow *Q* in a real word. (See Question 78, page 117, for more info.) So — no *Q*. (You've probably noticed that *Z* isn't there either.)

To play "Happy Birthday to You" on some phones, you can dial the area code first, and then press the following numbers to hear the "musical notes." (Some phones don't have notes associated with the numbers, so it doesn't work.)

112, 163
112, 196
110, 8521
008, 121

62.

Can you be electrocuted while on the phone in the bathtub?

This is not a recommended activity, but if you happen to drop your telephone into the tub, don't panic. You might get a bit of a shock, but you won't be electrocuted. That's because a phone doesn't carry a full electrical charge, like something that is plugged into an electrical outlet. A phone runs on a very small current, about 1/1000 of what would be needed to stop your heart. But it's best to be on the safe side — no chatting while you're soaking. Cell phones? Water is not suggested. Not much should happen to you, but you will definitely wreck the phone, and cell phones are expensive. Make your bathtime a peaceful, talk-free time, and save yourself the aggravation.

63.

What was the first e-mail?

Let's go back a bit first. The original idea of an Internet was to link university and government researchers together to make it easier and less expensive for scientists to collaborate on projects, to share data and to access one another's computers from afar. That's what Internet means: interconnecting computer networks. The U.S. Department of Defense did the first development in the 1960s. Originally it connected Stanford Research Institute, the University of California at Los Angeles and at Santa Barbara, and the University of Utah, through something called ARPANET, which stands for Advanced Research Projects Agency Network. The key to this collaboration was the ability to send mail electronically — e-mail.

In 1971 Ray Tomlinson, a computer engineer, sent the first e-mail message — to himself, on another machine in the room. If that isn't anticlimactic enough, he can't remember what it was he said! He figures it was QWERTUIOP or something like that. (That's the nonsense word you get when you type across the top row of a keyboard). At the time, Tomlinson was working for a company that had been hired by the U.S. Department of Defense to build ARPANET. He was tinkering with the idea of an electronic messaging program — so primitive at that point that it could only send and receive messages between people who were using the same machine. So it was a really big deal to send a message to *another* machine using ARPANET . . . even if it was in the same room. Tomlinson also came up with the @ symbol to tell a computer where to send a message.

For most kids nowadays, looking something up on the Internet or sending someone an e-mail is an automatic part of life. But this technology has completely changed the way people communicate with one another. Historians rank the birth of the Internet right up there with these three huge discoveries:

1   1844: Samuel Morse sends the first telegram: "What hath God wrought!"

2   1876: Alexander Graham Bell's first phone call: "Mr. Watson, come here. I want you."

3   1895: Guglielmo Marconi's first wireless transmission: "We speak across time and space. . . . May the new power promote peace between all nations."

"QWERTUIOP" wasn't much of a way to start the e-mail revolution, but there has been no turning back since that very first message.

- Throughout the world there are approximately 30 billion e-mails sent per day. This number is expected to double by 2006.
- Queen Elizabeth II sent the first royal e-mail message on March 26, 1976, announcing that the Royal Signals and Radar Establishment in Malvern was available on the ARPANET system.

Why are there no letters to go with the numbers *1* or *0* on a phone?

Phone designers kept the numbers *1* and *0* for what are called "flag" functions. The *1* is reserved for long-distance, and *0* is for dialling the operator. You will also notice that most area codes have a *0* or a *1* in them ("flagging" that you are dialling an area code).

65. Is there another way to regain energy other than by sleeping?

By e-mail

Nothing comes even close to the power of a decent sleep. You can last longer without food than without sleep. Scientists don't quite know why humans are programmed to need sleep, but it's about restoring the body. Sleep is the ticket; resting just doesn't cut it. Sleep researchers say it doesn't have to be eight hours of sleep in a row — as you get older, you tend to sleep in smaller spurts anyway. You also have to get into a deep sleep — that means reaching stage four of non-rapid eye movement (NREM) sleep — before there is a release of the growth hormone that lets your body restore itself.

Think you can beat the system and stay awake? Think again. Rats deprived of all sleep lived for only three weeks instead of the usual two or three years. In driving tests, sleep-deprived adults score as badly as, or worse than, drunks. Ask any new parent, or a student cramming for exams, about lack of sleep — it makes you punch-drunk and a little crazy. It would be nice if a cup of coffee or some other form of caffeine would help. In fact, it will give you a temporary energy boost, but it is not a replacement for sleep, and can actually interfere with it.

Sleep is by far the best method to *regain* energy, but there are ways to *conserve* energy too. Eating smaller meals helps. It takes a huge amount of energy to digest food and convert it to energy your body can use. That process is called metabolism. So if you eat a gigantic meal — especially a fatty one — even though you gain energy from the food you've just eaten, your digestive system (a BIG part of your body) becomes metabolically very active and you don't have as much energy (in the form of glucose) immediately available for other things. Your stomach has a big job to do, producing acid and pepsin to break down the food, and contracting rhythmically.

What knocks you out each night but doesn't harm you?
Sleep.
　　　　　　　　　　～

What do you call a sleeping bull?
A bull dozer!

Strange Sleep Facts

- The average person falls asleep in 7 minutes.
- We will sleep for one-third of our life — about 24 years on average.

Is there a real Sasquatch? Is there really such a thing as the Loch Ness Monster (Nessie)?

Shannon S., Surrey, B.C. and Cody McC., by e-mail

We don't know for sure. This is a great topic because people are so passionate in their convictions, either as believers about these amazing creatures or as naysayers about the whole phenomenon. This area of study is called "Cryptozoology," a delicious sounding word that means finding out about unknown, hidden or not yet classified animals.

There may indeed be such a thing as a Sasquatch or the Loch Ness monster. Over the course of history other rumours or tall tales of odd animals have turned out to be true. For instance,

the duckbilled platypus was considered a hoax when it was first discovered in 1797, and scientists thought the lowland gorilla was a myth until one was discovered in 1847. No one in the West believed there were giant pandas until 1913, when one was captured. And a coelacanth, a giant fish that scientists assumed had been extinct for 60 million years, was found in the net of a South African fishing boat in 1938.

It's always possible that Sasquatches and the Loch Ness monster are hoaxes, though. But there has been talk of a "Big Foot " or giant "wild man of the woods" since Europeans first came to North America. First Nations people have legends about two-footed giants from before that time. Most of the 450 or so sightings of the estimated two-and-a-half-metre-high Sasquatch are from the 1920s and the late sixties and early seventies in the Pacific Northwest (Washington and British Columbia). That includes some famous but controversial 1967 film footage, and continual sightings, even today, of some large furred beast, casts of its footprints and reports of its strong odour.

Sightings of the Loch Ness monster in the extremely deep and murky lake (loch) in northern Scotland have been reported for even longer — 1500 years! Those who believe in Nessie tend to think she is somehow related to the plesiosaurs, giant sea reptiles from the time of the dinosaurs, some 60 million years ago. In the past 150 years "she" has been reported to be salamander-like, have a neck like a horse, have a giant humped back, have a long tapering tail and an eel-like head, and be a "horrible great beastie." One report even had Nessie looking like a giant log that upturned a boat.

Maybe the Sasquatch and the Loch Ness monster really do exist — nobody has proven that they do or don't . . . yet.

67.

Many people say that Disney's Pluto was named after the planet Pluto. Is this REALLY true, or has that been made up?

Monica H.

Yes, it is true, and it makes sense when you know that the planet was discovered in 1930 — the same year that the animated dog first appeared. In the first Pluto film, *The Chain Gang*, Mickey Mouse was in prison and two unnamed bloodhound-like dogs were part of the posse that tracked him down when he escaped. This was very early in the Disney world. *Steamboat Willie*, the first Mickey Mouse film, was made just two years earlier, in 1928.

In 1930 the next Disney film, *The Picnic*, had "Rover" as Minnie's dog. Finally in *The Moose Hunt* (1931), Pluto got a name and a job as Mickey's sidekick. It takes a long time to make an animated film, so the Disney folks were likely in the middle of making *The Moose Hunt* when the planet Pluto was discovered.

The planet was named for the Roman god of darkness and the underworld. It was discovered by astronomer Clyde Tombaugh, who was following up on the work that another astronomer, Percival Lowell, had started before he died in 1916. The suggestion for the planet's name came from Venita Burney, a schoolgirl in Great Britain who won a naming contest. She picked Pluto because of the connection with the god of darkness and because the first two letters of the name are the same as the initials of Percival Lowell, who is really the father of this discovery.

There is a Lowell Observatory in Flagstaff, Arizona, named for Percival Lowell. It was founded in 1894 to look into whether life on Mars could exist. Scientists at the observatory discovered the rings of Uranus and numerous asteroids, and ultimately the planet farthest from our Sun, Pluto.

68.

What does the Queen carry in her purse?

This is a much-asked question. For a long while there was only speculation for an answer. It was always assumed that Her Majesty didn't need identification or taxi fare. *Majesty* magazine, an amazing periodical packed with all things Royal, suggested that she carries: a comb, a handkerchief, a small gold compact, a tube of lipstick . . . and on some Sundays, folded bills to put into the collection plate at church.

As part of the jubilee celebrations, Buckingham Palace answered a series of Frequently Asked Questions, and this was one of them. They said: "The Queen uses spectacles to read her speeches, and carries her glasses in her handbag. The Queen doesn't need to carry any money. The Keeper of the Privy Purse is the official manager of the Queen's money. He carries the Privy Purse, a heavily embroidered wallet, at the Coronation."

There you go, dull but true. But one can only suppose that Buckingham Palace wouldn't mention if the Queen also carried a paperback novel, or a list of the ninety-six two-letter words accepted in Scrabble.

69.

What was the first Web site?

Alysha M., Edmonton, Alberta

As we learned in the answer to question #63, ARPANET was the predecessor of the Internet. The best-used part of ARPANET was e-mail, which grew in popularity in the 1980s and early 1990s, along with newsgroups. That was, until Tim Berners-Lee, an English particle physicist and computer scientist, working at the European Organization for Nuclear Research, or CERN, in Geneva, Switzerland, finally figured out a way to share more information between teams of researchers. (CERN is the world's largest particle physics centre. It's where physicists look into what matter is made of and what forces hold it together.)

Tim Berners-Lee posted the first Web page at 2:56:20 p.m. on August 6, 1991. Unfortunately this site is no longer accessible, but CERN has a huge history of the World Wide Web on their own Web site, since they consider the work of Berners-Lee and his colleagues one of their greatest achievements.

Berners-Lee proposed the idea of the World Wide Web in 1989, and it came together within two years. His contributions are many, but the four critical things he developed are:

- ▲ the very first Web browser
- ▲ HTML, the coding system for documents
- ▲ HTTP, the way computers communicate with Web sites
- ▲ URL, the way we address things on the Web

Paul Kunz, a research scientist at the Stanford Linear Accelerator Center (SLAC) near Palo Alto, California, posted the first North American Web site on December 12, 1991. It consisted of three lines of text and two hyperlinks — not much to show off. But others caught on to the idea fast. After 1993, when the first browser, Mosaic, was introduced at the University of Illinois, the Web spread more quickly than anyone could ever have dreamed. By June of 1993 there were 130 Web sites. By the end of 1994 there were 10 000 *servers*. In 2003, just ten years after Mosaic, there were more than 1.4 billion unique Web sites.

■ **A group called Foundation Technologies has figured that the time it took various technologies to reach 50 million people was:**

Telephone	75 years
Television	13 years
The Web	4 years

How do they get the lines and logos underneath the ice at hockey games or skating shows?

If you have ever tried to flood your backyard to make a skating rink, you know that making a smooth, flawless surface is harder than it looks. Inside the concrete floor of an ice rink is a maze of pipes full of a liquid coolant. Its job is to make the concrete freezing cold, so that a good ice surface can be laid on top of it. The key to making good ice is keeping the temperature and humidity constant while you lay down the twelve or so layers of ice.

Take a hockey arena, for example. That ice is not naturally white. After the first layer of ice is laid down, the entire floor is painted using water-based white paint. Then the workers add another layer of ice, and the face-off circles and lines and sponsor's logo are painted on with stencils or by hand. (One trick is to freeze string into the ice to get the lines straight.) The third layer seals the paint, and then layer after layer the workers build up the ice until it is the desired thickness and hardness. The total amount of water used to build a regulation-sized rink is around 45 500 litres.

It turns out that hockey needs a cooler rink than figure skating — you weren't just imagining it if you have watched a live hockey game and shivered. Hockey players like harder ice (about −4° Celsius) than the figure skaters need (−2° Celsius). There are many reasons for this, but how the skate blade's edges react, and not having the ice shatter, are the most important.

Maintaining the ice is the next challenge. The ice-resurfacing machines (which are often called Zambonis after inventor Frank Zamboni) shave off the surface, bathe it with a spray of warm water and let the ice re-freeze into a clean, clear surface. Being the first to skate on clean ice is terrific.

71.

What do the military say when they are using the alphabet? I know *S* is Sierra and *Z* is Zebra, but what are the rest?

Morgan G., Richmond, B.C.

The Alpha–Bravo–Charlie alphabet is one of the best-known codes in the world. The International Communication Alphabet (ICA) and the United Nations' International Civil Aviation Organization (ICAO) code use these set words in place of each letter of the alphabet. This practice started with the U.S. military around 1955, and is used around the world by airlines.

The idea is that using standard words (like Alpha, Bravo and Charlie) makes it easier for others to recognize which letter you are trying to say, rather than just saying A, B, C. This works especially well when it is noisy, or if you don't speak English. Try saying "C" and "T" in a loud room — it's hard to hear the difference. Now try "Charlie" and "Tango." Easier, isn't it?

Here's the ICA:

Alpha	Juliet	Sierra
Bravo	Kilo	Tango
Charlie	Lima	Uniform
Delta	Mike	Victor
Echo	November	Whiskey
Foxtrot	Oscar	X-ray
Golf	Papa	Yankee
Hotel	Quebec	Zulu
India	Romeo	

Other organizations have developed their own alphabets from this original code. The New York City Police use: Adam Boy Charlie David Edward Frank George Henry Ida John King Lincoln Mary Nora Ocean Peter Queen Robert Sam Tom Union Victor William X-ray Young Zebra.

72.

What do you call a number like 1691 that reads the same upside down?

Really cool, and really rare. It's not a palindrome. That's when something *reads* the same backward and forward, such as 2002 or "Madam, I'm Adam." This is more like an upside-down palindrome, but there isn't a unique term to describe it. Mathematicians describe it using the concept of "rotational symmetry."

Impress your friends with this: the number 1961 is actually a "rotational symmetry of order two." That means that if you rotate it about its centre two times (each time 180 degrees), it gets back to its original position.

The Mercedes symbol, the Woolmark symbol, the recyclable symbol or an evenly formed green pepper sliced in half illustrates an order three rotational symmetry: it takes three turns of 120 degrees to get back to the beginning position.

A perfectly drawn plus sign (+) is an order four — four turns of 90 degrees get it back to its original position. A snowflake has an order 6 rotational symmetry — using 6 turns of 60 degrees.

The order of rotational symmetry of a circle is infinity. If you look at hubcaps, you'll notice that most of the designs on them have rotational symmetry of some degree.

Try to think of what would be the next number after 1691 that's an example of order two rotational symmetry. Give up? It works for 1881, 1961 — you figure out more. The numbers that work are *1, 6, 8, 9* and *0*, and the letters are capital *H, I, N, O, S, X* and *Z*.

Answer: 6090

106

73.

Vampires are corpses that come back to life — not ghosts — so why is it they don't have a reflection?

Whoa. First of all let us get the vampire story straight, as there are vampire myths from all over the world. Generally, a vampire is thought to be some sort of creature returning from the dead to make life for the living more of a challenge. There are actually said to be hundreds of kinds of vampires, with all sorts of powers, like changing shape, controlling the weather or controlling others' minds.

According to legend, there are dozens of reasons why someone might become a vampire. Here are a few:

- How you acted when you were alive: for example, if you were a very bitter person or if you practised witchcraft.
- How you looked: It could be the shape of your teeth, the colour of your hair or eyes, or whether or not you had a weird growth on the "tail" of your backbone. In the Balkan countries, redheads were thought to be vampires, and in early Greece blue-eyed people were suspected of ending up vampires too.
- Where you lived.
- How you died: Murder raises your odds of becoming a vampire, as does suicide. In Romania or Bulgaria, corpses who had a stake driven through their chests were almost certain to become vampires.
- If you were born out of wedlock.
- If a cat leaped over your grave.

You might think that all vampires wear long black capes, have sharp fangs and drink blood. If so, you likely got that image from the most famous vampire, Dracula, who showed up in a book written by Bram Stoker and published in 1897.

Heard of Vlad the Impaler? It sounds like a good name for an action figure, but in fact he was a fifteenth-century Transylvanian prince. His father was called Vlad of the Devil. The son was *Vlad Dracula*, or the Devil's son. This Prince Dracula, also called Vlad the Impaler, got his name from his nasty habit of impaling and mounting his enemies on stakes. Stoker was inspired to model his own fictional vampire on Prince Dracula.

And now to your question about a vampire's reflection. It was Stoker who started the idea that vampires have no reflection. Why? Here are a few things we know about Stoker himself:

- He knew about the age-old superstition claiming that mirrors capture a bit of your soul. Mirrors were also considered to be a way into the spirit world.
- We know that Stoker had had a dinner conversation with playwright Oscar Wilde about the difficulty of capturing the essence of a person's character and soul in a portrait. (Oscar Wilde went on to write about this in his novel, *The Picture of Dorian Gray.*) Stoker apparently resolved this difficult question by making his character, Dracula, have no reflection and therefore no soul.

What is a vampire's favourite soup?
Scream of mushroom!

74.

Why are carpenter pencils rectangular in shape instead of round or hexagonal like writing pencils?

MFPSAL, by e-mail

They are shaped like that so they won't roll away from where a carpenter is working. This flattened octagonal shape is so well-designed that it won't even roll off a slanted surface such as a roof. The other smart thing about this simple tool is that the wide lead can be sharpened to a chisel point that will last longer than the point on a round pencil.

Carpenters rarely use up their pencils, because they are made so well they can last a very long time. The lead is extra strong for making heavy marks and for surviving the worksite. Believe it or not, there are people who collect partially used or brand-new carpenter's pencils. That's because there's usually a logo of a lumber supplier or tool company on the pencils, which makes the various pencils popular with carpenters, collectors . . . and carpenters who are collectors.

75 • How would you make a disco ball?
Linda G., by e-mail

Disco dancing isn't dead. You can have your own dance party with one of those wacky mirrored orbs that reflect the light in a million different directions. Traditionally they are made of cut-up mirrors, but you can make one more safely, plus do it any size you want, for cheap! cheap! cheap! You know all of those CDs that come in the mail urging you to sign up for Internet access? This is a great recycling project for them.

Gather up the following:
▲ an adult to help
▲ a stack of unwanted CDs
▲ a big styrofoam ball
▲ tacky glue
▲ glitter
▲ white glue
▲ a small brush
▲ scissors
▲ masking tape
▲ a fishing swivel
▲ some fishing line

1. (Here's where you need that adult:) Cut up the CDs into random-sized pieces using scissors. There is no "right" way — just do what works for you. Or you could wrap a CD in a towel and smash it with a hammer.

2. Put a piece of fishing line around the ball and make a loop at the top. Use masking tape to hold the fishing line in place.

3. Using the tacky glue, place the CD bits as close together as you can, starting from the top of the ball.

4. When it is all finished, paint a light coat of white glue in the spaces between the CD bits and sprinkle the glitter onto the wet glue. When it is dry, shake the ball to get rid of the loose glitter.

5. Put the fishing swivel onto the loop and hang the disco ball at the desired height.

6. Dance the night away!

76.

Why is red considered Stop, green considered Go, and yellow Slow Down? Why isn't blue Stop, purple Slow and orange Go?

Jonathan C., the Kootenays, B.C.

Why not indeed? It seems random, but stoplights were purpose-built — designed with a purpose in mind. At the end of the horse-and-carriage era when cars came into the picture, traffic was a big mess with people stopping and going wherever and whenever they wanted. To bring some order to the roads, planners used the best idea they could come up with: copy what the trains were doing.

Railroads used red for Stop because in western cultures red has been a signal for danger, death and blood for thousands of years. Red seemed to be the obvious choice for Stop, but green and amber were just luck of the draw. Way back in the 1830s and 1840s when railroads had just gotten started, the colour for Caution was green, and Go was clear white. You can probably imagine the problems. If Go was white or clear, then occasionally when you saw any old white light, like a streetlamp, you might think it was a Go signal. One time a red glass lens fell out of a Stop sign, leaving the white light bulb. The train engineer, seeing the white light, saw Go when it should have been Stop, and his mistake resulted in a horrible crash.

Railroads came up with their current signal system — no white lights, just red, green and amber — none too soon. That way, any time they saw a white light they would know that something was wrong. Traffic engineers saw that the railway people had worked out the bugs in the system, and borrowed it for cars. The first traffic light was installed near the Houses of Parliament in London, England, in 1868.

The first electric traffic signals were installed in Cleveland, Ohio, in 1914. Planners thought they could get away with just red and green, but added the yellow for Caution a few years later because they needed to warn people that Stop was coming soon. Detroit, the home of automobiles, had the first modern four-way signals.

- How do colour-blind people distinguish red and green lights? They recognize the brightness, and know by rote that in vertical stoplights, red is on the top and green is on the bottom.

- If you're facing forward on a boat, the port or left side is marked with a red light, and the starboard or right side is green — you need to know the sides of the boat to follow the rules of navigating. (An easy way to remember which side is which is: *port* has four letters and so does *left*.)

77.

What's the difference between a second cousin and a cousin once removed?

Kelly M., Sayville, New York

When you figure this out, you'll be on the road to becoming an anthropologist. That's because anthropologists study kinship, and your cousins are your kin or relatives. I recommend making yourself a chart while you read this.

Let's start with some basics. In our culture,

cousins are the children of your parents' brothers or sisters. The children of your aunt or uncle are your first cousins. I'll give you an example. I have a cousin called Kimo Meikle. He is the son of my father's brother, so he is my first cousin. (He lives in Hawaii, hence the name.)

What does "once removed" mean? It has to do with the generations. Removed always involves the children of your cousins. Once removed is one generation "away." Twice removed is the next generation down. Kimo, my first cousin, has a son called Ethan, so Ethan is my first cousin once removed. If Ethan has a child (Kimo's grandchild), that child will be my first cousin twice removed.

To understand second cousins, let's go back to the term "removed," which always means a relationship with another generation. Second cousins, third cousins and so on are parallel to each other, so my son Mac and my cousin Kimo's son Ethan are second cousins to each other. If our children have children they will be third cousins to each other.

For the ultimate test, try combining the two. If your second cousin (your parent's cousin's kid) has a child, that child is called your second cousin once removed. The next generation after that child would be twice removed. Confused? Ask your parents.

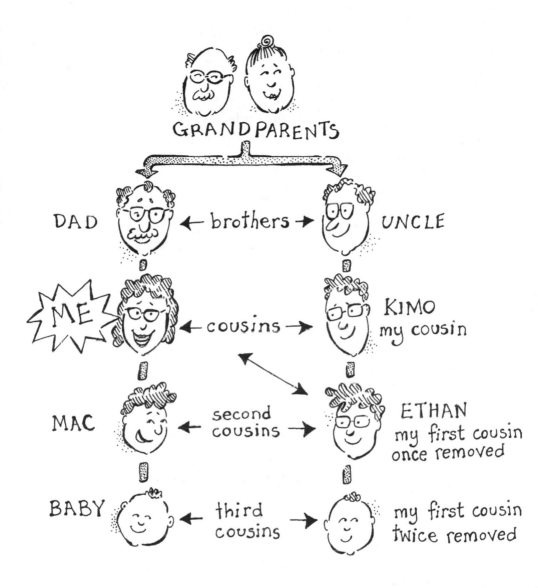

78.

Why does the telephone keypad have 1–2–3 at the top and the calculator has 7–8–9?

First there was the rotary phone, which started with *1* at about the "two o-clock" position, and worked counter-clockwise to *0*. And there was the calculator and cash register.

Have you ever watched someone like a bookkeeper run a calculator or adding machine without looking at the keys? Their fingers fly so fast you can't believe they're keeping track of the numbers. Calculators, the keypad on your computer keyboard and the cash register keypad all have a grid of numbers, with *0* at the bottom left and *9* on the top right.

So why make touch-tone phones essentially the opposite, with *1* at the top left and *9* at the bottom right? When Bell Labs started designing their newfangled touch phones they tried to find out why keypads had been designed in the order they were. It turned out that no one had done any research — it was pure luck that the keypad layout of the existing calculators and computer keyboards worked out so well for fingers. Bell figured that three rows and three columns of numbers was still the way to go, but made a significant change: starting with *1* at the top left. It was logical (that's how we read), it's the easiest to figure out, and there were fewer mistakes in "dialling" this way. Also, if you look at your phone keypad,

you will notice that there is an alphabet associated with the ten numbers (2=ABC, 3=DEF, etc.). This is because phone numbers used to include words. For instance, if you lived in Amherst, your number might have been Amherst 53, and you would dial it like this: AM 53 — or 2653.

Rarely are these different keypad designs a problem . . . unless you happen to be one of those people with flying fingers. Bookkeepers must get very frustrated when they "dial" a telephone. Newer machines such as automated tellers have used the phone keypad, perhaps just to keep folks on their toes.

79.

How do most ships and planes sink in the Bermuda Triangle?

Erin

Most ships and planes *don't* sink in the Bermuda Triangle, which is the area formed by connecting Puerto Rico, Miami and Bermuda. But back in 1964 a writer named Vincent H. Gaddis wrote an article saying that an unusual number of planes and ships had gone missing in this area. He came up with the name The Bermuda Triangle. Gaddis's work was fiction, but there had been reports of strange goings-on in the area for hundreds of years. Some people believe that a super-race living under the sea or possibly in space is responsible for these disappearances. Giving the area a name caught the public's imagination and added fuel to the fire. Here are a few claims about the Triangle:

- Christopher Columbus had weird experiences travelling through this area in 1492. His compass went wonky and the sailors saw odd lights in the sky.
- The earliest ship to disappear was the *Rosalie* in 1840.
- The first U.S. navy vessel to disappear was the USS *Cyclops* in March, 1945.
- The last known ship to disappear was the *Connemora IV* in 1956.
- Five Avenger fighter airplanes disappeared during a regular two-hour patrol flight from Fort Lauderdale, Florida, on December 5, 1945. This was right after they reported that things were looking strange and that their instruments were going crazy. Another plane tried to rescue them, having reported seeing an orange flash in the sky. It then disappeared too.

The Bermuda Triangle does have some scientifically proven oddities. There are only two places in the world where a magnetic compass will point to true north: the Bermuda Triangle and the "Devil's Sea" off the east coast of Japan (another area where weird disappearances are said to occur). And there are small, bizarre yet intense storms over the Gulf Stream that can brew, completely devastate the adjacent landscape, then clear up within minutes.

However, when investigators actually dug into the facts about all the accidents and the ships disappearing, they found no more occurrences in the Bermuda Triangle than in other places, and often the disappearances happened during big storms. Lloyd's of London, a huge international insurance company, determined that the area wasn't any more dangerous than other parts of the ocean.

What is the most common word
in the English language?

And Other WEIRD WORDS and PHRASES

What is the most common word in the English language?

Chris G.

It is "the" by a big lead. "The," like many of the rest of the words in the following list, are articles, which are used with nouns to limit or define that noun. They are not much of a word on their own, but imagine how difficult it would be to write even one sentence without some of the following words. They're listed in order (reading down), with the most common at the beginning:

the	his	when	them	time	way
of	they	we	then	could	find
and	at	there	she	no	use
a	be	can	many	make	may
to	this	an	some	than	water
in	from	your	so	first	long
is	I	which	these	been	little
you	have	their	would	its	very
that	or	said	other	who	after
it	by	if	into	now	words
he	one	do	has	people	called
for	had	will	more	my	just
was	not	each	her	made	where
on	but	about	two	over	most
are	what	how	like	did	know
as	all	up	him	down	
with	were	out	see	only	

In 1939 Ernest Vincent Wright wrote a book called *Gadsby: A Story of over 50,000 Words Without Using the Letter E.* (Seems he wasn't claiming that there was no *e* in the title.) He tied down the *e* key on his typewriter and went for it. Here is the first paragraph of his book:

> *If youth, throughout all history, had had a champion to stand up for it; to show a doubting world that a child can think; and, possibly, do it practically; you wouldn't constantly run across folks today who claim*

121

that "a child don't know anything." A child's brain
starts functioning at birth; and has, amongst its
many infant convolutions, thousands of dormant
atoms, into which God has put a mystic possibility for
noticing an adult's act, and figuring out its purport.

Eeeeeek!

81. Where did the saying "hold your horses" come from?

Nikul, Toronto, Ontario

Not surprisingly, this came from the equestrian world. When you want to keep your horses from getting too excited, you hold them still. If people want *you* to slow down they might say "Hold your horses," and they've been doing that since the 1840s. It's basically the equivalent of saying "Wait a minute!"

"Never look a gift horse in the mouth" is another horse expression that is "as old as the hills." Well, at least it is as old as the fourth century. Again horses figure here, since you check a horse's teeth to find out how old it is. Even if it looks like a perky young filly, looking at the teeth will tell an expert the truth.

You are showing horribly bad manners if you receive a gift and make insulting comments about it — just say thank you. St. Jerome, who came up with the saying "Never look a gift horse in the mouth," was reacting to people who were critical of some writing he had done for free. He was ticked off at their attitude, and was telling them not to make slighting remarks about something they'd been given.

82.

Why do you call the Queen's 50th anniversary the "jubilee"?

We call the Queen's fiftieth anniversary the "jubilee" because jubilees are celebrations that happen every fifty years. The word comes from the Hebrew *yobel*, (a ram's horn trumpet) which was blasted on Yom Kippur, the Day of Atonement, announcing the jubilee year. The Bible's Book of Leviticus lays it all out for the farmers of the time: farm for six years and take the seventh off for a sabbatical where you let the land rest (lie fallow), and after seven times this (forty-nine years) you take the fiftieth year for a jubilee, and don't work. Let the land go fallow, pay off your debts, free your slaves, and generally forgive everyone. The trumpet heralds a year of grace.

For the last seven centuries the Roman Catholic Church made every twenty-fifth year a "jubilee year" for forgiving people and making things right in people's business and personal life. The last jubilee year was 2000.

The British Royals have had many occasions to celebrate jubilees. There have been a number of British monarchs who reigned at least half a century: Henry III, Edward III, James VII, George III, Queen Victoria and Queen Elizabeth II.

Queen Victoria celebrated her reign with both a Golden (fifty years) Jubilee in 1887 and a Diamond (sixty years) Jubilee in 1897. She became Queen in 1837, when she was eighteen years old, and reigned until 1901.

83.

What does the expression "raining cats and dogs" mean?

Mirissa K., Minitonas, Manitoba

"Raining cats and dogs" means it's raining extremely hard — so hard, in fact, that with the rain and wind it might even sound like a cat and dog fight.

The phrase has been around since 1708. Apparently humorists and cartoonists back then drew cats and dogs falling from the sky and added pitchforks and shovels. And there are other expressions that conjure up the same sort of vivid images: raining blue blazes, raining cat poles, raining blue thunderbolts, raining bullfrogs or raining heifer yearlings.

Different theories on this rather peculiar saying have been tossed about. Here's one: A few hundred years ago, few cities had garbage collection. Instead, all kinds of junk, including corpses of dogs and cats, were simply thrown into the streets, where they would pile up in the gutter. That pile up was called a kennel. A really violent rain would dislodge the dead cats and dogs from the kennel and sweep them along the street, thus "raining cats and dogs." Very yucky . . . but very interesting.

If you don't buy that theory, another has to do with Nordic mythology. Cats, who are often said to have unusual powers (witness witches and their black cats), were also thought to have great influence on the weather.

Also, the dog and the wolf are both symbols of wind. The rumble of dog growls can sound like rain and thunder. In old pictures, wind was sometimes depicted as the head of a dog or wolf, out of whose mouth came blasts of wind. Both animals were attendants of Odin, the Norse storm god.

So back to the phrase, "raining cats and dogs." The cat could be taken as a symbol of the downpouring rain, and the dog of the strong wind that comes with a rainstorm. Even today when English sailors see an unusually frisky cat, they say, "The cat has a gale of wind in her sail."

It can't *really* rain cats and dogs, but over the past two hundred years there *have* been recorded cases of raining frogs, fish, stones, grain, seeds, salamanders, worms, straw, lizards, mussels, hazelnuts, leaves and green slime. While such occurrences have often stumped scientists, they figure that rainstorms, waterspouts or small windstorms called whirlwinds have swept up these items and poured them back down again on unsuspecting, umbrella-toting people.

What's the worst weather for rats and mice?
When it's raining cats and dogs.

84.

Where did the term "OK" come from?

Nupur

This has to be one of the simplest but most widely used expressions. Too bad its history isn't as easy.

OK is definitely American, and it is not short for *Okay. OK* was a jokey way of abbreviating "oll korrect," which is itself a jokey way of saying "all correct." (This was probably a funnier joke if you had been there around 1839. Spelling things wrong in a goofy way was a fad then.) *OK* was a common sort of shorthand at the time, because people also used abbreviations like *PDQ* for "pretty darned quick" — the way we use *LOL* for "laugh out loud," *BTW* for "by the way" and *FYI* for "for your information" today. Most of the silly acronyms are long gone, but *OK* stuck, and it still means all correct.

85. Why do we say "An elephant never forgets"?

We say it because we think elephants remember their keepers or their trainers. But it was actually the Greeks who first said it a different way: "A camel never forgets."

About a century ago elephants somehow got in on the act. Elephants have a fifty or sixty-year life span, plus they have a long memory and are well known for recognizing people and other animals. In 1910 the popular author Saki coined a phrase about elephants he'd seen while growing up in Burma: "Women and elephants never forget an

126

injury." It quickly became truncated to "Elephants never forget," and became part of popular language. There is even a song from 1934 called "The Elephant Never Forgets."

How do you make an elephant float?
Ginger ale, ice cream and one elephant.

~

Why don't elephants like playing cards in the jungle?
Because of all the cheetahs!

Why is the last car of a train called a caboose?

Not because it rhymes with *vamoose*, which would be such a lovely explanation. Like many word origins, this one is a bit unclear, but there are some good theories. One is that it comes from two Dutch words: *kaban huis* (for ship's galley or cabin house or shelters to protect the crew's fireplaces), which eventually got mixed into one word: *kabuis*. But Texans claim the word originated there. They say that *caboose* is an Americanization of *calabozo*, a Spanish word meaning *jailhouse*, which is another small enclosed space. How that translates into the wooden shanty at the back of a long freight train, from which a conductor oversees the train's operation (and cooks his meals), seems to be lost . . . although the trips were long and the conductor or trainmen might have felt like they were in jail.

What we do know is that *Caboose* began to be used in the western part of North America around 1859. It was similar to the sort of space for the crew that you'd find on a ship. In the east, that car was called a way car, cabin car, crew car, crummy, shanty, brakeman's cab, train car, accommodation car or conductor's van. *Caboose* is used in the west today, and *way car* is still often used in the east.

87.

What do you call the plastic things on the end of shoelaces?

Mrs. Galbraith, St. Benedict School

They are called aglets. The word comes from the Latin *acus*, which means an ornamental pin or needle. You get the idea that perhaps aglets were a lot more interesting in the fifteenth century than the snippets of plastic or metal we get on our shoelaces today. In fact, it is really an aglet if it is decorative; a more utilitarian tip is often called a tag.

The eyelet is the hole through which a lace is threaded (led by the aglet). Actually, the word *aglet* is also the term for any decorative pins or studs on your clothes, but we don't really use it for either, very often.

What do you call these commonly found symbols?

¥: yen

¢: cent (You knew that, right?)

$: dollar (But you didn't know that the $ was used long before the U.S. dollar, did you? It's likely from the figure 8 for Spanish "pieces of eight.")

€: euro (the newest currency)

What do these currency symbols have in common? They are all letters with one or two strokes through them.

Here are more symbols:

©: copyright

#: octothorpe, referring to the eight points. It is sometimes called *pound* in North America, usually referring to telephone keypads. In musical notation it is a sharp.

@: at (originally a shortcut for the Latin *ad*, which was commonly used in price lists of goods)

/: forward slash, stroke, solidus, oblique dash or virgule

\: backslash

&: ampersand, often used as the word *and* in signs or logos. It comes from the Latin *et* meaning *and*. "Scripty"-looking letters for the *e* and the *t* were combined, to make the new symbol &.

*: asterisk, from the Greek word for a small star, *asterikos*. An asterisk is a five or six-pointed star, indicating to the reader to look at the bottom of the page for a footnote or a short explanation. (When you are playing the piano, ∗ points out where you should use the pedal.)

~: tilde has various meanings, but on a keyboard it is used for an accent in Spanish and Portuguese languages. And on a website URL it indicates a personal page.

89.

Why do we say, "There's a frog/toad in my throat"?

Jeannette R., St-Claude, Manitoba

Is it because of that raspy, throaty sound of your voice? Back in the Middle Ages, if you had an infected throat, doctors might put a live frog into your mouth, head first. When the frog inhaled, it was supposed to get rid of *your* infection by taking it into *its* own body. We don't practise this odd procedure any more, thank goodness, but the saying is still used to mean hoarseness.

90.

What is a *lb.*? If you say "pounds," why is the abbreviation *lbs.*?

Megg M.

Here's a secret — there's a good chance that answers to word origin questions are eventually going to go back to Latin roots, where much of the English language came from in the first place. And, bingo, that's the case here. *Pound* comes from the Latin word *pondo* or *pondus*, for weight. Dig a little further and you'll find out that the symbol £ and the *lb.* abbreviation are for *libra,* which is Latin for *pound.* So *libra pondo* means a pound in weight.

Now the tricky thing is why the British used the £ symbol for their currency. It was the symbol for the British pound sterling, and had been called that because the Roman pound (which was 340 grams or 12 ounces) of pure silver would make 240 silver pennies. The pound sterling was divided into 20 shillings or 240 pence (12 pence to the shilling).

When Great Britain shifted to the decimal system (using a base of 10 versus 12) in 1971, they just kept the name *pound.* It was hard enough for the people to give up their shillings, farthings, sixpence and half-pennies — giving up the pound would have created even greater strife. So now the £ is divided up like a dollar, with 100 pence = 1 £. The coins are 1p, 2p, 5p, 10p, 20p, 50p, £1 and £2.

91. Why do we say we are "pooped"?

Eirian, Vancouver, B.C.

We say we are pooped when we are exhausted, too tired to move or bone weary. And we've been saying it since about 1934. But *why* do we say *pooped?* Likely *pooped* comes from the nautical verb *poop,* which is when a sailing ship has taken in a lot of water over the stern, onto the poop deck, (the partially raised deck at the stern or back of a ship). One term for a huge wave over the stern is a *pooper.*

And *poop* is the right word for that deck too, because long ago, sailors would rig a little structure aft of the deck so they could hang over the ocean and . . . relieve themselves.

But back to *pooped.* Whenever a big wave swamped the ship, at least temporarily stalling it, the ship was said to be pooped, meaning something that is stopped, not moving anymore, exhausted. *Poop* is also used in the expression "to poop out" or to run out of steam. And of course a "party pooper" is someone who won't get into the big happy mood of a party — he or she has no energy and poops out. Oh, poop. There is also a famous Chuck Berry song worth having a listen to, called "Too Pooped to Pop."

Other words for extreme fatigue are: burnt out, keeled over, tuckered out, run ragged, bushed, knackered, on your last legs, out of it and zoned.

92.

Who came up with the question mark and the exclamation mark?

You can find both *?* and *!* used all over the world, even in China (since 1912) and Japan (1868). But in Spanish, both signs are inverted and placed at the beginning of a sentence, like this:

¿Que pasa?   ¡Hola!

It wasn't really anyone in particular who invented the funny little squiggle over a dot to indicate a question. Here's how it came about: *questio* in Latin meant "a seeking"; it eventually came to be used for an inquiry. It was put at the beginning of a sentence that asked a question. Seven letters is a lot to devote to that function, so after a while it was shortened to *Qo*, until the day that the scribes (remember, there were no typewriters or computers back then) made it even smaller by putting a *Q* over a tiny *o*. Over the years this then became a squiggle over a dot, and eventually worked its way to the end of the sentence too.

Questio ➞ Qo ➞ Q ➞ ?

What about the exclamation mark? Same idea. The Latin *Io* was for an "interjection of joy," and the *I* came to be put over the *o* until the *I* was over a dot: !

Io ➞ I ➞ !

134

For a single mark, *!* has a lot of things going for it! It is terribly expressive! It can show all kinds of emotions and states of mind — surprise, wonder, contempt, disgust, regret and absurdity! But use it sparingly, because using *!* too often lessens the impact considerably!

92 1/2.

What is the dot over the letter i called?

Tyler B., Hildale, Utah

Here's a short answer for a short question. It is a super-script dot, called a *tittle* or an *i-dot*. There are also those who call the dot a *jot*.

93.

What are the two-letter words you are allowed to use in Scrabble?

Memorize these, and Scrabble insiders say you can increase your score by 30–40 points a game:

The 96 Two-Letter Words Allowed in Scrabble
aa ab ad ae ag ah ai al am an ar as at aw ax
ay ba be bi bo by de do ed ef eh el em en
er es et ex fa go ha he hi hm ho id if in is
it jo ka la li lo ma me mi mm mo mu my
na ne no nu od oe of oh om on op or os ow
ox oy pa pe pi re sh si so ta ti to uh um un
up us ut we wo xi xu ya ye yo

Some of their definitions are quite scientific or exotic, but they *are* real words.

needles

plate

star

column

dendrite

column capped with plate

Why does snow sparkle?

And Other Nifty Facts About the NATURAL WORLD

94.

Why does snow sparkle?

Here's a hint: What else sparkles like snow? Crystals. In fact, it would be more accurate to call snowflakes by what they really are: snow crystals. And a snow crystal is simply an ice crystal. Each crystal is formed when the water vapour on particles of ash, dust or pollen inside a cloud freezes. What defines a crystal is the way the molecules line up in a hexagonal lattice formation, so every crystal has six sides. Every snowflake is different, but they can be sorted into crystal types, which vary because of the temperature and humidity occurring when they formed. An International Commission on Snow and Ice came up with a classification system for solid precipitation in 1951. They defined seven principal snow crystal types: plates, stellar crystals, columns, needles, spatial dendrites, capped columns and irregular forms. And there are three more types of frozen precipitation: graupel (which look like round pellets), ice pellets and hail. Frozen raindrops are called sleet.

Frozen crystals can combine to make a snowflake that looks as if it's made of just a few crystals, or like a puffball with thousands of tiny mirror-like sparkling crystals. A snowflake's sparkle occurs when light reflects off the many angled surfaces and catches your eye.

Snow sparkles most when it is fresh — melting dissolves that property. When snow melts, all the surfaces dissolve and the crystals lose their shape. The result is fewer angled surfaces to catch the light ... and the snow loses its sparkle.

The largest snowflake ever recorded was 20 x 30.5 cm. It was reported to have fallen in Bratsk, Siberia, in 1971.

Why does the ocean have salt in it and how did it get in there? About how much salt is in the Dead Sea?

Ciara M., Ontario, Emeka U., by e-mail
and Lindsay W., Whitesboro, New York

The salt in the ocean is a far cry from your average table salt. It is actually a very complicated solution containing more than fifty natural mineral salts. Sodium chloride (table salt) is the most abundant, with much lower concentrations of others such as calcium salts (calcium carbonate or lime, and calcium sulphate), potassium salts (potassium sulphate) and magnesium salts (magnesium chloride, magnesium sulphate and magnesium bromide). Plus there are dissolved sediments and rocks from the ocean floor, decayed matter and water. Dissolved salts are carried to oceans from rivers and streams — to the tune of almost 4 billion tonnes a year.

Scientists think that the total amount of salt in all the oceans may be almost 50 million billion tonnes. Most seawater has a salt concentration of thirty-five parts per thousand, which means that 3.5% of seawater's weight comes from the dissolved salts.

The exception to the 3.5% ratio is the Dead Sea, which is actually a salt *lake*, not a sea. It is up to ten times as salty as the oceans, and is located on the very lowest point of the earth's surface, about 400 metres below sea level. It is called the Dead Sea because nothing — not even seaweed — can survive in the water or around the shore, which is white from the salt crystals that cover it. If a fish swims into the lake from one of the streams that feed it, the fish dies instantly. This incredible lake got so salty because the Jordan River and some small mountain streams feed it, but there is no drainage out of it. The only way water can leave the lake is through evaporation, and that makes the salt even more concentrated.

Most table salt comes from mines rather than from salt in the sea. Sometimes iodine is also added to it to prevent an enlarged thyroid gland called a goiter. Since manufacturers began adding iodine to table salt, goiters are rarely seen in industrialized or first world countries, but they are still common in developing nations.

How old is the oldest living thing that is still living?

Zachary M., by e-mail

It's nothing cute or fuzzy, nor is it a relative of a dinosaur or a gorgeous prehistoric-looking plant. The oldest living thing is probably — get this — some bacterial spores that were found in 2000 near Carlsbad, New Mexico. The spores (genus *Bacillus*) were floating in liquid brine inside a salt crystal. Perhaps the find isn't too exciting sounding to us, but it is a *huge* discovery to scientists. They calculated that the salt likely dates back about 250 million years, and it looks like these spores are ten times older than anything ever discovered before. But, as with all scientific claims, these records have to be independently substantiated.

The bacteria is called 2-9-3, which isn't much of a name for something that may help to uncover the beginnings of life. So far, the scientists know that the same kinds of crystals were found in a meteorite in 1999. They also know that both

Jupiter's moon Europa and the planet Mars at one time had oceans, and possibly the same kind of salt formations.

By the way, these bacteria could win the age race by hundreds of millions of years. Before 2000, the best contender for "oldest living thing" was some 25 to 40-million-year-old bacteria which were found inside the stomach of a bee encased in amber. You may wonder just what scientists were doing inside that stomach. Well, they were looking for the oldest living thing.

The oldest living thing that you can actually *see* (bigger than bacteria) appears to be a Tasmanian bush, commonly known as King's Holly (the only species in existence of *Lomatia tasmanica*). It has been dated by researchers at over 43 000 years old.

97 ◆ Is soapstone really soap, and if so, then can it be used like bathroom soap?

Stephanie M., Cambridge, Ontario

Soapstone isn't soap at all. (Doesn't this kind of thing drive you crazy?) There is usually some vague connection between two words like this. In this case it is because soapstone has a bit of a soapy/slippery feel.

Even weirder is the fact that soapstone is mostly made of talc, the *softest* of minerals. Talc gets a 1 on the Mohs Scale of hardness; diamonds rate a 10:

1 Talc   6 Orthoclase

2 Gypsum   7 Quartz

3 Calcite   8 Topaz

4 Fluorite   9 Corundum

5 Apatite   10 Diamond

It turns out that miners and drillers use the term "soapstone" for any rock that has a soft soapy/slippery feel, whether it has talc in it or not.

While you can't use it as bathroom soap, there is a small chance your sink or countertop might be made of soapstone, since it makes beautiful fixtures for bathrooms and kitchens. But in truth, since you hardly want a sink that gets scratched every time a pot or fork touches it, a "soapstone" sink is likely made of steatite. That's a harder rock (3 to 4 on the Mohs Scale) and is 40% or so talc. Soapstone can also be used for fireplace surrounds because another of its qualities is its ability to absorb and distribute heat evenly.

Many Inuit carvings are said to be made of soapstone, but in fact most are made from steatite or serpentine, both harder than soapstone.

What have we learned from this soap/soapstone puzzle? Often things aren't what you think they are, or as they are labelled. Keep asking questions!

98.

What exactly are Mexican jumping beans anyway?

They're from Mexico, and they do jump, but they're not really beans. What we call a Mexican jumping bean is actually the seed capsule of the shrub *Sebastiana pavoniana*. It's a fairly ordinary shrub with dark green leaves that turn red in the winter months, but those seed capsules or "beans" make it something special. These little beans can writhe around, rolling and hopping like a happy puppy in a roomful of Ping-Pong balls.

What's really happening is that a type of moth that is particularly active while hatching has hatched a marketing sensation. The female small gray moth, commonly known as the jumping bean moth (*Laspeyresia saltitans*), lays eggs on the flowers of the shrub. When the eggs hatch, the tiny larvae dig into the seed capsules, eating out parts of the interior and living there until the end of the summer. At that time the seed drops to the ground, since it can't produce a flower without some of its crucial parts. Then the hollowed-out seed containing a healthy fat moth larva starts jumping around. The warmer it is, the more the larva — and therefore the bean — jumps.

Then as the weather gets colder the larva spins a cocoon around itself and cozies in for the winter months. It is becoming a pupa now and it stops jumping. The next spring the pupa pushes out of the capsule through a hole it cut the fall before (while it was still jerking around), and becomes a moth.

Once just a simple act of nature, Mexican jumping beans have metamorphosed into a big export item over the years. As pets go they are pretty interesting, not too expensive, and you don't have to feed them. But timing is everything when buying this item. The beans will wiggle and groove for weeks or even months in their container (if they have air — punching holes in the lid of a shoebox or jar will do it). By putting them on your hand or any other warm object you can get them jumping even faster. But as the larva begins turning into a pupa, your purchase becomes rather useless. Suddenly you'll have a crop of moths, but unless you have jumping bean shrubs in your garden for the moths to lay their eggs on, so that the cycle can continue . . . no more jumping beans. So enjoy the novelty, because it doesn't last long.

99.

How do mood rings work?

As fads from the 1970s go, the mood ring was right up there with the pet rock for silliness and for massive but short-lived sales. Basically, a mood ring is a heat-sensitive liquid crystal "quartz" stone that changes colour according to your mood. Or so the producers would have you believe. (Notice that only one colour shows any glee in your life, so they should have been called "Moody" rings.) Here's what the colours were supposed to show about your mood:

blue:	**happy happy**
greenish-yellow:	**dull**
purple:	**moody, erratic**
reddish-brown:	**insecure**
black:	**desperate, down, gloomy**

Joshua Reynolds invented the mood ring. He was a marketing guy who later developed the ThighMaster. Reynolds was a student of biofeedback (a way of controlling your body's reaction to stresses) and called the mood ring a "portable biofeedback aid." A widely read astrologist wrote about the rings, so when they went on sale, the public went crazy. Fall of 1975 saw 15 million mood rings sold, from $5 knock offs to $250 gold versions.

In truth, body temperature makes the crystals change colour — the warmer your body, the happier you were said to be (or so your blue ring indicated). The fad was all over in a matter of months, which was a good thing because the liquid crystals tend to stop working after a couple of years. Mood rings do come back into vogue occasionally. The more contemporary versions are made of better material, and last longer. The original rings turned black for good very quickly.

Index

Index

ridges, 29
  witches', 29
mirror, 109, 110-111
mistletoe, 72
Moh's Scale, 143
mollusc, 41
mood ring, 146
moon landing, 91
Morris, Desmond, 39
Morse, Samuel, 94
mule, 13
muscle, 21
  piloerector, 25
  sphincter, 28
NASA, 91, 92
nerves, 17, 32
nervousness, 30
New Year's Day, 69
nightjar, 9
nipples, 29
non-alcoholic, 54
nostrils, 5, 8
nuclear disarmament, 75
Odin, 124
okay, 39, 126
oligosaccharides, 45
Oscars, 76-77
oxygen, 20
  oxidation, 55
pain, referred, 32
palindrome, 106
panda, giant, 99
parasympathetic nervous system, 28
Parliament, 68
peace symbol, 75
peanut butter, 49-50
  allergies, 50-51
  Carver, George Washington, 50
pencil, carpenter, 109-110
peppers, hot, 58-59
  Scoville, Wilbur, 58-59
  Scoville Unit, 58-59
pepsin, 97
phosphorus, 59
Pilgrims, 67
platypus, 29, 99
plesiosaur, 99
plum pudding, 85
Pluto, 100

poop deck, 132
Pope Gregory the Great, 86
potassium, 57, 59
potato chip, 52-53
  Crum, George, 52-53
preservative, 71
protein, 45, 50
puberty, 29
Queen Elizabeth II, 95, 101, 123
Queen Victoria, 123
railroad, 112
razor, 35-36
reaction, involuntary, 30
Reard, Louis, 78
red, 41-42
  traffic light, 112
red carpet, 41-42
rest, 6, 96
Reynolds, Joshua, 146
Roosevelt, Theodore, 67
root beer, 54
rotational symmetry, 106
royalty, 41-42
Russell, Bertrand, 75
Saint Jerome, 122
Saint Nicholas, 66
Saki, 126
salary, 71
salmonella, 7
salt, 71
  Dead Sea, 140-141
  ocean, 140-141
  table, 140-141
  thyroid gland, 141
Santa Anna, Antonio
  Lopez de, 47
Santa Claus, 65-66
  Mrs. Claus, 66
  Sinter Klaas, 66
sapodilla tree, 47
Sasquatch, 98-99
sassafrass, 54
sayings,
  "an elephant never forgets," 126, 127
  "break a leg," 83
  "frog in my throat," 131
  "hold your horses," 122
  "never look a gift horse in the mouth," 122

"pooped," 132-133
"raining cats and dogs," 124, 125
Scoville, Wilbur, 58-59
  Scoville Unit, 58-59
Scrabble, 136
sebaceous gland, 55
sebum, 22, 23, 55
seed, 61
semaphore, 75
Shar-pei, 22
shaving legs, 35-36
shock, 93
shoelace,
  aglet, 129
  eyelet, 129
Siamese twins, 17-18
sign language, 38
skin cells, 19, 26
sleep, 6, 96-97
  caffeine, 97
  deprivation, 96
  non-rapid eye movement, 96
smoking, 27
sneezing, 86
Sniglet, 53
snow,
  melting, 139
  snowflake, 139
  sparkle, 139
soap, 142-143
soapstone, 142-143
sonar system, 3
soul, 86, 87, 109
speed of light, 65
speed of sound, 65
spices, 71
spore, bacterial, 141
stern, ship, 132
stockings, 36
Stoker, Bram, 108-109
stools, 111
stratum corneum, 22
sugar, 71
sunlight, sensitivity to, 27
superstition, 40
  cat, black, 124
  evil eye, 87
  fig sign, 88
  stairs, 84
  theatre, 83

150

Photo by Lionel Trudel

Marg Meikle, also known as The Answer Lady, lives in Vancouver with her husband Noel, the ever-inquiring Mac (age six) and Rosie the border collie (age eight). Marg's favourite people are librarians and kids who ask good questions. Her favourite colour is red, she's keen on many crafts, but her current passion is painting with acrylics.

Other books by Marg Meikle, filled with more fascinating facts, are *Funny You Should Ask* and *You Asked for It!*

Trademarks

The following trademarked names have been used in this book:

Beano, Big Mac, Cheetos, Chiclet, Coca-Cola, Coke, Frito-Lay, Mercedes, Ping-Pong, Scrabble, ThighMaster, Velcro, Woolmark, Wrigley's Juicy Fruit, Wrigley's Spearmint